To Hear Your Voice

Written Verse of the 21st Century
Inspirational and Motivational

Carol Kappes

Olympus Story House

In Dedication To:

My family and children
My relatives and close friends
My social networking connections
My readers
And to LinkedIn and Google

Contents

Preface

We all view the world we live in differently; from the eastern to the western world and across the ocean. I see the world in 'God's eyes'; and I viewed it this way ever since high school. With my simple beginnings on the farm in the Midwest of the United States of America, and my academic education, my life experiences, my observations, my career as a licensed dental assistant in four-handed dentistry with pediatric and general dentists; working with a diverse group of patients and my knowledge of the spiritual world came about these written verses.

I envision a changed world, where we can be more understanding as the internet and the social networking had come about and drawn us together. You are about to read the compilation of these verses in sequence of birth to death in all aspects of life, similar with Maslow's theory. Maslow's theory is actually factual in the way I had lived my own life. You will find special meanings and messages in them; and some will change your thoughts on ways to see things in a different perspective.

It was those quiet moments in the day where many divine aspirations came about and I quickly had to jot them down so as not to lose them. I am an emotional/expressive writer that gets in the heart and minds of people or their core being. The essence of nurturing the human being into full growth to prosperity and a meaningful life is truly important for everyone's emotional well- being. We all have a spirit within ourselves to accomplish what we were born to do.

An Author of Verse.
Carol Kappes

Life

The Miracle Of Human Creation

Conception needs to take place
    Doesn't always happen

Uniting of cells and divisions
    Doesn't always stay

Growth must occur and continue
    Doesn't always adhere

Systems must be in working order
    Doesn't always be accurate

Birth process begins by contractions
    Doesn't always stay well

Baby arrives into the world
    Doesn't always know its departure

Carol Kappes 2012
Inspired of human creation

A Mother's Joy

There was a joyful day in
October with the arrival
Of a baby girl. She joins
Two brothers at home.

The moment she was held;
A precious child had been
Protected in her Mother's
Arms so tightly wrapped.

A daughter welcomed and
Loved, a gift sent from above;
To cherish in the minutes and
Hours of her newborn life.

A treasure within the family.

Carol Kappes 2013
In honor of Mothers
Around the world.

Daddy's Girl

I loved my Dad;
I wanted to be near him.
And one time he had been
Fencing in the fields.

I asked if I can see Dad.
Mother told me not to go,
But I did anyway!

I walked right into the
Barbed wire fence and
Somehow it swung back
At me very fast.
Faster than I can blink!

Anyway, my chin now
Shows scars from that day.
I was rushed to the doctor
To place some stitches.

Once again; I went with Dad
Shopping for groceries.
I helped unload them from
The car and accidently shut
My thumb in the car door.

Another trip to the doctor
For stitches to my thumb.
Yes, I was daddy's girl!

To this day I often remember
My love for my Dad with
A memory that I hold dear.

Carol Kappes 2012
In honor of Fathers around the world

A Gifted Child

Listens and obeys parents
Respects neighbors and others
Does thinking daily
Learns to problem solve
Takes in a lot of nature's beauty
Enjoys the simple things
Learns the spiritual side
Learns understanding
Loves to read and write
Learns to be responsible
Learns to have discipline
Learns to be organized
Learns a craft and hobby
Sees the joys and sorrows
Learns to observe people
Can read their eyes and mind
Is clued in on body language
Watches people's traits
Knows right from wrong
Learns about emotions
Knows about poverty and wealth
Learns about society influence
Enjoys helping others
Learns about teamwork
Learns about hard work
Enjoys being educated
Manages self-development
Strives towards set goals

Overcomes any weaknesses
Gains bravery and courage
Predicts and visions the future
Learns and uses intuition
Develops common sense
Senses when body needs care
Knowledge of inner peace

Carol Kappes 2013

When You Hear the Word "Colors," What Do You Think?

I think of the colors of crayons
I think of the colors of markers
I think of the colors of pens/pencils
I think of the colors of toys
I think of the colors of the rainbow
I think of the colors of fruit
I think of the colors of vegetables
I think of the colors of paint
I think of the colors of dye
I think of the colors of fabric
I think of the colors of shoes
I think of the colors of clothing
I think of the colors of make-up
I think of the colors of yarn/thread
I think of the colors of the earth
I think of the colors of flowers
I think of the colors of cars
I think of the colors of houses
I think of the colors of the people's skin
I think of the colors of the nations' flags

Show your vivid colors in the way you live!

Carol Kappes 2011
Inspired of elementary students

You Are. . .

What you eat

What you hear

What you watch

What you read

What you say

What you drink

What you wear

What you feel

What you think

Need improvement?

Carol Kappes 2011

Riding a Bike In Life

Biking for adventure
Going into the unknown
Learning to get on
Facing life forward
Looking way ahead
Trying to stay on
Working out the stumbles
We took the fall strong
Willing to get back on
Having more patience
Balance remains stronger
Speed improves with practice
Agilience takes hold
Accomplishment done
Reached the destination
On the road towards success
The journey was great!

Carol Kappes 2012
Inspired of first
Bike lessons

These Most Useful Books

The only books you really need
For a child after he learns to read-
The encyclopedia and dictionary;
Along with newspapers and magazines.

Why? You ask. Let me tell you. This
Is the source of information for their life.
It is used for studies, skills and knowledge.
This is what will drive their interests.

The other important book of value
When a student is in high school
Is the Holy Book or the Holy Bible;
Along with instructions of faith in Him.

Why? You ask. Let me tell you. This
Is the source of information for their love.
It is used for character, morals and understanding.
This is what will drive their motivations.

Carol Kappes 2011
Inspired of simplicity and practicality
Realize various cultures of religion

I Can Only Love You For Now

As you are becoming a teenager
As you are becoming independent
As you are becoming into maturity
As you are witnessing good and evil
As you are becoming an individual
As you are becoming lawful in society
As you are becoming well educated
As you are making the right choices
As you are gaining an employment
As you are becoming a safe driver
As you are becoming more responsible
As you are becoming a man or a woman
As you are witnessing the world
As you are becoming a mindful citizen
As you are becoming your own character
As you are becoming your own freedom

Carol Kappes 2011
Inspired by the
Teenage years

A Farmer's Daughter

My father toiled the land, and loved the land;
He grew corn, soybeans, oats, and alfalfa.
Lived on an acreage of home and buildings,
Raised dairy cows, hogs, chickens and ducks.

Life was spent in doing everyday chores,
Going to school and learning all studies.
Caring for the family; preparing meals of
Fruit and vegetables grown from the garden.

My beginning was started on the farm in Iowa;
A Midwest state in the United States of America.
I've grown to love the land and all of natures'
Magnificent beauty, in my little corner of the world.

Then I left home for work in the city
To begin an adventure of my very own.
Many thoughts still take me to the wonder
Of how my life has been truly blessed!

Carol Kappes—2011
Born and raised in Iowa, USA

I'd Like To Thank You

I'd like to thank you for spending time with me
I'd like to thank you for helping me understand
I'd like to thank you for all of your sacrifices
I'd like to thank you for taking care of me.

I'd like to thank you for giving me a life
I'd like to thank you for your guidance
I'd like to thank you for your protection
I'd like to thank you for loving me.

I'd like to thank you for all your prayers
I'd like to thank you for all of your worries
I'd like to thank you for your wisdom
I'd like to thank you for helping me.

I'd like to thank you for accepting me
I'd like to thank you for teaching me
I'd like to thank you for remembering me
I'd like to thank you for being my parents.

Carol Kappes -2011
Inspiration of Parents
Dedicated to my Parents
LS and RS

The Best Gift We Receive

First, we receive and accept it
It is wrapped beautiful and tight
We begin to wonder about it.

Slowly we begin to peer in and look
Then we begin to see and understand
We feel happiness and excitement.

We acknowledge and thank the Giver
For the most wonderful gift of love
One where memories will remain.

Carol Kappes 2013
Inspired of Gifts received;
As well as the Christ child

Nature

Life's Beauty

Everything in life has its place
    Just as noticeable as a trace.
When we follow along each pace
    We often wonder what we'll face.
Continuing on as if we're in a race
    We should take the time to say grace.
Every moment, in any particular case
    Reflects beauty; as flowers in a vase.

Carol Kappes 1987

Silver Lake

Nestled in the upper Midwest
Where the Canadian geese flock-
An awesome sight to behold
When down the path I walk.

Eager to watch and be noticed
The geese sound their little honks,
Waiting for a hand of corn seed
As residents begin the new day.

Looking out into the scenic lake
I take notice of the silver lining,
Reflected by the sun's shiny light
Of the mid-morning sky of gray.

The sidewalk path near my car
Was filled with goose droppings,
But beyond that mess I had left
The etched memory in my mind.

Carol Kappes 2011
Inspired from college/technical years
In Rochester, Minnesota USA

Nature

Today I journeyed out beyond
To capture scenes that I'm so fond.
The melting snow causing water trickles
And added rain that just drizzles.

With help from the bright, warming sun
The days quickly go on, one by one.
Soon there'll be a new growth all around
As nature begins without a sound!

Carol Kappes 1986

I Walked Thru a Rose Garden

I look for the beauty

The scent captivates me

The colors refresh and stimulate

The thorns show hurt we endure thru life

The blossoms fade away upon age

It is simply elegant

Carol Kappes 2012

Each Day a New Beginning

Look towards a bright beginning
Take each moment as a prize;
Relish the scenes around you
Enjoy the sounds and then explore.

What might you find interesting?
Cherish it in your mind and heart
See the beauty that it has to offer
Enjoy the time you have with it.

Each day comes and then it goes
With each breath it keeps you alive.
Witness the chance to take it in
As tomorrow the day starts to begin!

Carol Kappes 2011

Life Begins Anew

I watched the rain
Clean up the dirt
Left from melting snow,
As spring came forth.

I see the crocus bloom
Amongst the cold ground;
A sight for our eyes
To witness once again.

I savored the scene in my
Mind this moment, and
Realized that beauty comes
When life begins anew.

Carol Kappes 2011

Think Of Yourself As a Blossom. Why?

It appears and springs forth into the world

It grows continuously with sun, warmth and care

It needs attention and protection in development

It shows beauty in its detail and character

It displays the vivid color in its silhouette

It requires refreshing water for its brilliance

It can withstand powerful winds and storms

It grows into maturity that sets fruit for others

It leaves a mark of depth and beauty while it's here

It tries to last, but wilts away in its chosen time.

Carol Kappes 2011

Purple Martins

Purple martins are such wonderful birds.
Just watching them swoop and sing
    Is such a splendid thing!

They keep the yard free
Of mosquitos and pests
    As they feed their young inside the nests.

We see them through two seasons
And when they fly back
    It suddenly signals autumn weather to unpack.

It's sad to see them leave,
But when spring arrives
    We'll be waiting in anticipation for their surprise!

Carol Kappes 1985
Inspired by their arrival
Year after year at the farm

Men In Flight

Look up into the blue sky
You see a plane so high

I often always wonder why
A pilot so willing to fly?

Their family makes a sigh
As passengers say goodbye.

Please don't let out a cry
Or tears will fall from my eye!

Look up into the blue sky
You see a plane so high

Carol Kappes 2012
Inspired from networking
Dedicated to pilots

The Storm's Path

I had been in the path of the storm:

> To face it
>
> To endure it
>
> To brace it
>
> To feel it
>
> To witness it
>
> To brave it
>
> To clean it
>
> To remember it

Carol Kappes 2013
Inspired of life's storms
Or difficulties you face

Emotion

Feeling Good

Walking helps keep one in shape
It's an exercise most anyone can take.
After a good night's sleep, you'll awake
And munch on a nutritious grape.

Feeling great and anxious for the day
Gives one opportunity for reaching success.
With your whole body being free from stress
You'll always be happy along life's way.

Carol Kappes 1986

Compliment

You look beautiful
I like your smile
You look young
I like your eyes
You look great
I like your legs
You look gorgeous

You look handsome
I like your tie
You look good
I like your outfit
You look happy
I like your strength
You look confident

Carol Kappes 2013
Dedicated to M
Inspired of giving
Someone a compliment

Emotions

Runs deep as parts of the river
Can be wild and out of control
Can be forced upon like the wave
Rushed violently as in a storm
Initially becomes very exhausted
Then becomes sullen and calm
Overcome by silence and peace

Carol Kappes 2012
Inspired by emotional feelings

Bitterness

Like the taste felt on your tongue
Like the way that people treat you
Like the weather being so cold
Like the experience of a scold

Carol Kappes 2013

Peace

Peace of the mind:

Peace in families

Peace in the schools

Peace in society

Peace of wrong-doing

Peace unto all souls

Peace from corruption

Peace from violence

Peace of hostility and war

Peace amongst all people

Peace amongst all nations

Peace treaty signed

Peace in the world

Peace within you!

Carol Kappes 2011
Inspired for World Peace-
Learn personal responsibility, conflict management,
And character building skills

Love In Short Supply

I think lots of people
Need love in this world.
It's in short supply.

Why? What happened?
Where did it go? When?
Are we looking for it?

It really must be found
As soon as possible.
I'm feeling so afraid.

People are lonely, sad
They're in conflicts; due
To emotional instability.

A love lost, will crumble
A love found, will repair
A love held, will remain

Carol Kappes 2012

A Sharp Tongue. . .

Pierces the ears

Often loses control

Uses demeaning words

Makes accusations

Tends to scold

Wants to restrict

Quenches any desire

Shows distastefulness

Offers no remorse

Carol Kappes 2012

Feeling Sad...

Not feeling like myself
More like a depression
Low feeling of sadness
Want to run from it all.

Nothing seems to go right
I'm taking the "fall."
Feels like getting nowhere
Hopelessness is in sight.

It doesn't seem to help
No matter how hard I try
I did the best that I could
My mind will not escape this.

Carol Kappes 2012
Inspired of depression

Handle With Care

We always talk about:

A bruised apple
A bruised cucumber
A bruised mango
A bruised pear
A bruised strawberry
A bruised tomato

But what about?

A bruised child
A bruised emotion
A bruised hurt
A bruised personality
A bruised spouse
A bruised soul

Carol Kappes
Inspired of injustice
Unfairness

Hate Is a Strong Word-

I hate you

I hate what you did

I hate what you said

I hate what you have

I hate doing this job

I hate that I have been chosen

I hate that I have been mistreated

I hate the weather today

I hate that some are lucky

I hate that some have it easier

I hate this assignment

I hate that person for some reason

I hate to wear this outfit

I hate to go to the party

I hate to hear your side

I hate to ....

Try not to use it!

Carol Kappes 2011

What Hurts In Loneliness Is. . .

A feeling that you're not loved
A feeling that you're not wanted
A feeling that you've done wrong
A feeling that you're not invited
A feeling that you're not pretty
A feeling that you're hopeless
A feeling that you're in poverty
A feeling that you're homeless
A feeling that you're empty inside
A feeling that you're not capable
A feeling that you're rather odd
A feeling that you're unable to try
A feeling that you're inadequate
A feeling that you're incompetent
A feeling that you're not lucky
A feeling that you're worthless
A feeling that you're helpless
A feeling that you're anxious
A feeling that you're depressed
A feeling that you're overly shy
A feeling that you're overweight
A feeling that you're losing friends

Carol Kappes 2011

Love Conquers All

I learned that
Through the struggles,
Through the pain.

One thing remains...

Love of God and others
Helps take it away,
Day by day.

Carol Kappes 2011

I Cried

So hard that I needed a dry
Wash cloth to wipe my tears.

I was missing you so much
That it hurt inside of me.

Memories came so sudden
Of many loving moments.

My heart felt so empty
Without your pouring love.

I've never felt so alone
As when you've left me.

Carol Kappes 2011
Inspired of loneliness
Spouse away on business,
Death of spouse/family/friends,
Break-ups

Memories

I spent the other evening thinking about you
And my—did I feel so blue!
Tears surfaced, rushing down my face
When reflections of you came into place.

Being apart, I often realize
Your life with me was a wonderful surprise!
How we cherished those happy moments together
Will stay with me now and forever.

Carol Kappes 1986

Venture

To My Son, I Love You!

As you step beyond ahead
You'll think of things I've said.
With every day that you face
You'll be going at your pace.

Take the future, move along
As your life is like a song.
With each melody you'll hear
As life changes in the year.

Keep your head up high
As you reach toward the sky.
For success is yours to take
As you celebrate with a cake.

Remember that thru the years
Your Mom had shed some tears.
She wants you to stay ahead
In the game of life, as you tread!

Carol Kappes 2011
In Dedication to DRK, my son
Farmington High School Graduate-June 8, 2012

To My Daughter, I Love You!

I have loved you ever so much
With my business world as such;
I felt that I didn't have time
To love you in your prime—

But with each passing day
My guilt lessens with each ray;
As I see your independence
In your plans that make sense.

Remember always to take pride
In everything that comes in stride;
Your college years are the best
As life unfolds with each test.

My love for you remains true
Always when I think of you;
You now have the same chance
To take on life with one glance.

Carol Kappes 2011
In Dedication to MRK, my daughter
Farmington High School Graduate- June 7, 2013

Graduation

Just as a plant takes root and grows,
So, too, may your dreams and goals.

The years ahead leads to a path
Of accomplishments and setbacks.

Follow the road built of strength,
Determination and perseverance.

It leads to so many possibilities;
And the blessings from God above.

Carol Kappes 2013

To the Graduate

As you begin "to do your part of
Deeds that begin within your heart."

May your graduation be a start-

> Of dreams coming true
> Of goals being reached
> Of success sliding in
> Of happiness shining through
> Of prosperity taking place

In the future you're about to face.

Carol Kappes 1987

Life's Moments

Of all the things in life I've seen
Memories come often in between.
The times of parents curving you
In directions worth steering through.

Going north, south, east or west
It doesn't matter, whichever is best,
To reach the chance and the desire
Whatever your heart begins to fire.

Strangely enough, it becomes most certain
That when it's the last final curtain,
Life was patterned in such a way
That it brightened with every passing day!

Carol Kappes 1987
Inspired of duty after Graduation

Those Golden Years

Many parents are becoming olden in years,
And it sometimes brings my eyes to tears.

Their life becomes limited in what they've done
To raise up their children that are already gone.

It soon becomes our turn to watch and care for them
And we'll realize then, they were precious as a gem.

Carol Kappes 1986
Dedicated to my parents
LS and RS, with love

The Olympics

The beauty of the athlete

The beauty of the sport

The beauty of the gracefulness

The beauty of the strength

The beauty of the agility

The beauty of the performance

The beauty of the sportsmanship

The beauty of the competitiveness

All because of persistent practice

Carol Kappes 2012
Inspired of Summer Olympics
London, Great Britain

May I? May You!

May I ask you for a favor? May you help me with this!

May I be your friend? May you have a great time!

May I have this dance? May you enjoy the evening!

May I borrow this today? May you bring it back!

May I come along, too? May you be very careful!

May I forgive you? May you always be happy!

May I take care of you? May you have a great day!

May I always love you? May your wishes come true!

Are we asking? Or expressing!

Carol Kappes 2011

Two Forces

God or Satan?

Love or hate

Light or dark

Sunny or gloomy

Good or bad

Truth or lie

Peace or evil

Blessed or cursed

Strength or weakness

Wise or foolish

Innocent or sinful

Eternal or condemnation

Life or death

Heaven or hell

Make the right choices!

Carol Kappes 2013
Inspired of the forces that
People choose in their life

To Hold On To:

Your commitment and goal

Your energy and stamina

Your passions and desires

Your enthusiasm and fun

Your curiosity and interests

Your uniqueness and life

Your willpower and authority

Your influence and leadership

Your character and personality

Your strength and courage

Your mentality and intelligence

Your spirituality and faith

Your wisdom and understanding

Carol Kappes 2011

We All Have a VOICE

Arguing, demonstrative, gossiping, criticizing, name-calling,
Swearing, complaining, bullying, blaming, bragging, shouting,
Attacking, insulting, screaming, groaning, opinionated,
Constructive, moaning, boisterous, scolding, crying,

Mourning, grief, sorrowful, preaching, advising, speaking,
Consulting, describing, directing, discussing, communicating,
Praising, singing, explaining, coaching, talking, mentoring,
Teaching, cheering, chatting,

Sympathy, praying, rejoicing, proclaiming, loving, accepting,
Approving, grateful, thoughtful, complimentary, joyous, greeting,
Humorous, laughter, jubilant, whistling, humming, hushing, sighing,
Whispering, signing, breathing.

Be careful how you use it!

Carol Kappes 2011
In collaboration

Duty

The Duties In Life

Making a jigsaw puzzle into a picture
Is a duty of searching, finding,
And placing.

Making a dream into a goal
Is a duty of effort, determination,
And achieving.

Making a frown into a smile
Is a duty of concern, kindness,
And caring.

Making a house into a loving home
Is a duty of time, patience,
And understanding.

Making a journey into a lifetime
Is a duty of love, family,
And working.

Carol Kappes 1987

Good

Be good

Pray good

Look good

Dress good

Talk good

Listen good

Act good

Feel good

Smell good

Study good

Work good

Prosper good

Live good

Stay good!

Carol Kappes 2013
Inspired of the
"Art of growth"

I Took the Time To:

Say a prayer

Help someone

Feed the hungry

Give to charity

Say hello

Visit the sick

Donate blood

Visit the elderly

Forgive someone

Tutor the child

Say thanks

Care for someone

Reflect on life

Smell the roses

See the beauty

Gather the bounty

Watch the rain

Hear the thunder

Witness the rainbow

Enjoy nature

Watch the sun set

Gaze at the stars

Give a smile

Honor our soldiers

Love one another

Enjoy the sun

Forgive the person

Clothe the naked

Listen to sounds

Read the scriptures

Volunteer

Enjoy life

Know thyself

Know others

Carol Kappes 2011

Take Responsibility-

To your manners

To your behavior

To your thoughts

To your duties

To your actions

To your discipline

To your work

To your problems

Carol Kappes 2012
Inspired of being responsible

Dancing Christmas Trees

Here we go to the car wash
And see the dancing Christmas trees
See them at our windows
Doing a ballerina dance.

Swish swashing the car so clean
Making it all so bright
Sparkling in the moonlight
As we drive away.

Carol Kappes 2002
In collaboration
With my two children

Mistakes

Admit it

Learn from it

Correct it

Remedy it

Straighten it

Then continue on!

Carol Kappes 2012

I Can't Keep Silent. . .

What happened to discipline?

What happened to ethics?

What happened to conduct?

What happened to obedience?

What happened to rules?

What happened to service?

What happened to duty?

What happened to honor?

What happened to morals?

What happened to behavior?

What happened to self-control?

What happened to values?

What happened to professional?

Carol Kappes 2012
Inspired of incident of Secret Service, USA
(Duties and professionalism towards work)

Life As Little Steps

Each step forward brings you adventure
Each step backward brings you doubt

Each step speedy brings you confidence
Each step slower brings you weakness

Each step skilled brings you pride
Each step skipped brings you pain

Each step higher brings you curiosity
Each step lower brings you deficiency

Each step reached brings you success
Each step pulled brings you failure

Each step to the right brings you joy
Each step to the left brings you hope

Each step up brings you energy
Each step down brings you lazy

Each step jumped brings you happiness
Each step slipped brings you sadness

Each step in the light brings you courage
Each step in the dark brings you worry

Each step hopped brings you excitement
Each step tumbled brings you depression

Each step on pavement brings you strength
Each step on quicksand brings you frailty

Each step danced brings you unity
Each step still brings you unrest

Each step upward brings you wealth
Each step downward brings you poverty

Each step risen brings you heaven
Each step fallen brings you hell

Carol Kappes 2011

I'm Proud

You've made it to kindergarten
You've passed your elementary
You've made it thru junior high
You've graduated high school.

Then you established your career
With either work or college years.
Spend time discovering yourself
And then take your next journey.

You've made it this far along
You've chosen to be single or
You've chosen to have a family
You've made your commitment.

Then you gained much understanding
With the experience you have had.
Spend it with pride your knowledge
And it will enhance your future.

Carol Kappes 2012

I Value. . .

I value your love and friendship
I value your smile and happiness
I value your joy and excitement
I value your care and companionship
I value your words and conversation
I value your help and responsibility
I value your advice and knowledge
I value your peace and understanding
I value your time and commitment
I value your skills and proficiency
I value your work and employment

Carol Kappes 2011
Inspired by networking
In Dedication to MSK

Are You Listening?

It gives you guidance
It gives you ideas
It gives you information
It gives you knowledge
It gives you perspective
It gives you motivation
It gives you opportunities
It gives you understanding
It gives you intelligence
It gives you encouragement
It gives you abilities
It gives you insights
It gives you strength
It gives you courage
It gives you improvement
It gives you productivity
It gives you confidence
It gives you interest
It gives you worth
It gives you wisdom
It gives you importance

Listen carefully!

Carol Kappes 2011

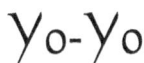

Yo-Yo

It has its up and downs and
Can be difficult to continue;
Sometimes can't get back up.

It works on continuous movement.
One misstep and it will fail; it
Needs precise attention, and action.

It is mastered by the hands
In top shape performance
Of rhythm, motion, and speed.

Mind, hand and eye coordination
Makes it possible to continue;
A skill to acquire in your life.

Carol Kappes 2012
Inspired of development,
Play and learning

Appreciate

Your talents and strengths

Your family and friends

Your health and wealth

Your values and morals

Your awards and honors

Your distinction and success

Your work and ethics

Your home and country

Your life and experiences

Carol Kappes 2012
Inspired by the gift of gratitude

Role

Working Towards
Our Financial Health

Begin with a budget plan
Communicate with partner
Consider the costs
Is it really needed?
Ask if it's necessary
Look for discounts; sales
Don't buy if wanted
Balance your checkbooks
Pay credit cards monthly
Reserve 10-20% to savings
Give some for charity
Begin an investment
Plan for unexpected job loss,
 medical needs, repairs
Plan for retirement
Discuss future needs

Will bring us to financial wealth!

Carol Kappes 2011
Inspiration from my Father

Words Of Thought

Nice to meet you
That looks good on you
How are you
You look well today
I've missed you
Thanks for listening
You've been helpful
That was a great idea
Excuse me
It was my mistake
I'm sorry
I didn't notice that
Hope you understand
Thanks for the advice
I really appreciate it
I forgot all about it
I'll keep this in mind
That was kind of you
You're welcome
You're a team player
We learn everyday
That's a good effort
We reached our goals
That was great advice

I never thought of that
You were right
You've done a neat job
You gave it your best
That turned out okay
It was more than I expected
It looks really nice
You're so thoughtful
Your responsibility shows
You made me feel better
I'm glad that we met
It was nice talking to you
Take care of yourself
Have a great day
Come again soon
I'll see you again
Thanks for the visit

Carol Kappes 2012
Inspired by
"What we say to others"

With All Due Respect

Respect the elders

Respect your parents

Respect the teachers

Respect the ministers

Respect the coaches

Respect the leaders

Respect your employers

Respect the landlord

Respect the neighbor

Respect your spouse

Respect one another

Respect yourself!

It shows with honor

Carol Kappes 2011
Inspired of respect

Great Leaders Show:

Responsibilities

Moral standards

Decision making skills

Good judgment

Listening abilities

Understanding

Gratitude and respect

Duty and obligation

Dedication to career

Knowledge and wisdom

Concern for others

Leadership accountability

High standards

Performance

Accomplishments

Achievement

Carol Kappes 2012

Communicate. . .

By mail in a letter, of notes written in ink

By parcel in a box, gifted and wrapped

By newspaper, checking out news and weather

By animals, for protection and guidance

By camera, sending pictures to loved ones

By Morse code, electric telegraph sent

By radio, playing music and news

By Braille, reaching out to the blind

By chalkboard or smart board; view presentations

By telephone, hearing their voice message

By television, viewing the news and shows

By walkie-talkie, a transceiver for messages

By microphone, talking out to the crowd

By fax, sending and showing information

By cell, seeing text messages written

By computer, checking the e-mail sent

By mobile device, use of GPS and internet

By webcam, seeing live video

By laptop, chatting and sharing interests

By mobile phone, talk, text, and use of apps

Carol Kappes 2011

Find the Key To:

The vehicle, the door, the locker, the trunk, the mail box,
the safe, the map

Their commitment, their happiness, their love, their heart,
their joy, their passion

Your endeavors, your goals, your wealth, your health,
your life, your soul

Don't lose it!

Carol Kappes 2011

Be Ready For Unfortunate Events:

A traffic accident
A medical need/emergency
A force of natural disasters
A career that ended
A death in the family
A catastrophe that happens
A failure that occurred
A mindful event

And be financially prepared!

Carol Kappes 2013
Inspired of future events that occur

Sergeant

I shall today salute you
For the great job you do!

Serve, honor, and protect
I do give you such respect.

You have courage and strength
To place yourself on lines' length.

The rigorous training you kept
Was definitely worthwhile yet!

Carol Kappes 2012
Dedicated to NC
Inspired of the military

If It Hadn't Been For- (Start-ups)

The Internet

LinkedIn

A Foreign Friend

My Inner Voice

Thinking of Others

Previous Writings

Google

My Circumstances in Life

This blog would have never came to be.

In conclusion to the year 2011; this blog is dedicated to all my readers and loved ones. Without you, life would have been difficult for me this year. I owe it all to YOU! Because you had cared.

Carol Kappes 2011
Carol's Corner
Inspired by the Ideas/
Process of Start-ups;
Steps/years are involved.

Where Is Our Strength?

It is seen in our physical muscles
It is seen in our mental mind
It is seen in our confidence
It is seen in our enduring energy
It is seen in our use of religion
It is seen in our influential trait
It is seen in our constant bravery
It is seen in our teamwork effort
It is seen in our continued growth
It is seen in our charity to others
It is seen in our leadership ability
It is seen in our work performance

Carol Kappes 2011

Bravery

Is when you "take the bullet"

Is when you "handle the situation"

Is when you "take the first step"

Is when you "tell your mind to do it"

Is when you "bury your anxieties"

Is when you "took the risk"

Is when you "get that first experience"

Is when you "show your responsibilities"

Is when you "succeeded to carry on"

Is when you "challenge yourself"

Is when you "ask the question"

Is when you "make that decision"

Is when you "help someone"

Is when you "have the courage"

Is when you "endure it"

Is when you "overcome your struggles"

Is when you "start taking control"

Is when you "have confidence"

Is when you "suffer through your crosses"

Is when you "manage your fears"

Is when you "conquered the battles"

Is when you "learn something new"

Is when you "get involved"

Is when you "stop worrying"

Is when you "start to believe in yourself"

Is when you "become emotionally stable"

Is when you "stand up for something"

Is when you "start over again"

Is when you "overcome some tragedy"

Is when you "have the strength"

Carol Kappes 2013

Regress

Why All the Violence?

What happened to the loving?
What happened to the sharing?
What happened to the caring?
What happened to the helping?
What happened to the earning?
What happened to the working?
What happened to the confessing?
What happened to the teaching?
What happened to the listening?
What happened to the learning?
What happened to the mentoring?
What happened to the talking?
What happened to the praising?
What happened to the thinking?
What happened to the encouraging?
What happened to the praying?
What happened to the giving?
What happened to the creating?
What happened to the advising?
What happened to the studying?
What happened to the tutoring?
What happened to the parenting?
What happened to the volunteering?

Keep your mind busy and stop hurting others

Carol Kappes 2011
Inspired for keeping the mind busy
With crafts, school, college,
Career, and retirement

You Gave Me a Lift;
When I Felt Down. . .

By your genuine spirit
By your helpful support
By your loving kindness
By your caring smile
By your magical touch
By your encouraging voice
By your wonderful thought
By your sympathetic ear
By your passionate soul

And then you turned me around.

Carol Kappes 2012

Why Is Sorry the Hardest Word?

Sorry tells the person that you still love them
Sorry lets them know you were mistaken
Sorry gives an apology or that you regret it
Sorry equals the balance you show for others
Sorry makes you become a better person
Sorry lightens the heavy load on the heart
Sorry helps the soul grow from within you

Make it into the easiest word!

Carol Kappes—2011
Inspired of forgiveness

You See the Child's Pain?

You can see it in their eyes
You can hear it in their cries
You can see it in their hunger
You can find it in their face
You can see it in their clothes
You can see it in their feelings
You can see it in their tears
You can find it in their temper
You can see it in their discomfort
You can find it in their thoughts
You can find it in their actions
You can see it in their injury
You can hear it in their language
You can find it in their attitude
You can see it in their sorrows

Carol Kappes 2011
Inspired to protect our children

Why Are We Fighting?

Put aside your argument

Put aside your hatred

Put aside your malice

Put aside your anger

Put aside your conflicts

Put aside your disputes

Put aside your cheating

Put aside your hostility

Put aside your profanity

Put aside your bullying

Put aside your meanness

Put aside your lying

Put aside your lateness

Put aside your carelessness

Put aside your greediness

Put aside your quietness

Put aside your coldness

Put aside your differences

Put aside your sinfulness

Put aside your treachery

Put aside your jealousy

Put aside your motives

Put aside your belligerence

Put aside your opposition

Put aside your laziness

Put aside your disagreement

Put aside your procrastination

Put aside your irresponsibility

Put aside your unwillingness

Put aside your resentment

Put aside your wickedness

And talk about it!

Carol Kappes 2011
Inspired of difficulties in
Families, Communities, Nations

What Will It Take? To-

Rid evil into good
Rid immoral into moral
Rid hate into love
Rid negative into positive
Rid misery into joy
Rid abuse into care
Rid poverty into wealth
Rid crimes into harmony
Rid wrong into right
Rid sin into grace
Rid profanity into ethics
Rid suffering into elation
Rid hunger into abundance
Rid unlawful into obedience
Rid outcast into worker
Rid handouts into prosperity
Rid graffiti into painting
Rid slums into apartments
Rid pollution into cleanliness
Rid waste into recycle
Rid problem into solution
Rid sadness into happiness
Rid lie into truth
Rid anger into compliance
Rid war into peace
Rid greed into content
Rid despair into hope

Carol Kappes 2011

What Is Pain?

Is a natural event when birth arrives
When you touch something hot
Is the dysfunction of a family
Is experienced when love has ended
Is acted upon by natural disasters
Any unrest, wrong-doing, injustice
It happens when hunger strikes
It occurs due to mental anguish
Is caused by careless decisions
When feelings/emotions are shattered
The loss of one's employment
When the human spirit is lost
It occurs against someone's will
Any betrayal, false claims, terrorists
Happens in illness, disease, and accidents
Anything caused by fire or explosions
Taking away a person or thing
Is a profound grief when someone dies

We have to endure it.

Carol Kappes 2011
Inspired by Friend

Struggle

We struggle to breathe

We struggle to survive

We struggle to live

We struggle to cope

We struggle to heal

We struggle to listen

We struggle to understand

We struggle to accept

We struggle to maintain

We struggle to weather

Carol Kappes 2012

I Tried. . .

To limit drinking

To stop smoking

To limit TV

To stop gambling

To limit computer

To stop swearing

To limit eating

To stop yelling

To limit spending

To stop worrying

To limit shopping

But it all takes willpower!

Carol Kappes 2011
Inspired of our choices
For a better lifestyle

Excruciating Physical Pain

Shows that you're vulnerable

Dampens your spirits

Cuts like a knife

Can start the flow of tears

Thinking becomes lessened

Lose interest of material things

Mind directed on the pain

What steps are taken next

Remembering your loved ones

Flashback to survival

Carol Kappes 2012

The Pain of Sin

Disobedience

Rebellion

Temptations

Sexual immorality

Wickedness

Destroys people from God

Carol Kappes 2013
Inspired of a sinful world;
People turning against God

Peace In the Works

In order to have peace, you must...

Take action on it

Know about it

Speak about it

Discuss on it

Reasons of it

Effects of it

Welfare of it

Collaboration of it

Value of it

Outcome of it

Wonders of it

Tranquility of it

For humanity and society

Carol Kappes 2013
Inspired of Geneva, Switzerland
Conferences that are happening
In Fall of 2013

World

Why Is There Hunger In the World?

Where does it begin? Why is it happening?
First of all—we need the agriculture to produce.
Feed your people in your nation-the crops that
Naturally grow there. Import as needed.

It happens due to economics and jobs of people.
Do they make enough? Are more people able to
Work and nation can prosper? If they are capable,
Help them find work. They would appreciate it.

God said the birds will survive. And to do that
They must gather seed, build a nest, and feed
Their young. As people, we are to do the same. Set
An example to get only what is mostly needed.

Our world has enough food to go around—it is the
Development and progress that needs to take place;
So that when people say grace, all the bounty of the
Land will grow and prosper as God had implied!

Carol Kappes 2011
Dedicated to FY

What Are We Doing In Today's World?

Anything on earth can be destroyed in a second! Take a look at the destruction-It can be done in two ways-

1. Destroyed by nature-Tsunami, hurricane, earthquake, tornado, hail, lightning, floods, etc.

2. Destroyed by man-Use of weapons, guns, bombs, explosions, fire, drugs, abortions, etc.

There is little we can do to stop the destruction by Mother Nature; except to teach and warn of your safety!

There is a lot we can do to stop the destruction by Man; to help make this world a better place for all of us to live!

The questions we need to ask are plenty. As leaders, we all need to take a stand for what is morally right.

Are we protecting our children, our children's children, and future generations?

Are we stopping the violence, terrorists, traffickers, criminals, corruption, and immoral thoughts?

Are the leaders fully capable, responsible, moral, and listen to their people's words?

Are we doing all we can to educate, inform, teach, and show responsibilities at home and in the schools?

Are we being neighborly to our people with compassion, kindness, and respect?

Are we serving the needs of our people in the family, community, society, country, and world?

Are we moving ahead with new insights to make life easier, or have we slipped off the path?

Are we sharing our interests to many others so that knowledge becomes deeper?

Are we moving forward in advances and others are being left behind?

Are we doing all we can to feed the hungry, impoverished, wounded, and sick?

Are the needs met of all people in the World with food, shelter, clothing, medicine and love?

Are we emotionally connected to the happiness in our land, city, state, and country?

Are we becoming too selfish, or self-centered that we are forgetting the future needs of others?

Are we becoming too materialistic that we only think about our own enjoyment of it, and not share with others?

Are we all seeking a spiritual side for guidance to help us make the right choice or decision?

Are we praying or meditating for peace, joy, love, wisdom, righteousness, purity, in our people?

What happens when we neglect the basics of man's heart, soul, mind, and strength? We become weak in love, divine grace, personality, character, stamina, energy, and outlook!

What then, you ask? We as a society has learned so much knowledge into the 21ˢᵗ century—**and man is destroying what God intended to be so beautiful!**

Why destruction by Mother Nature? Are they coming more frequent? Maybe it's to get our attention and to once again become caring to one another, loving, feeling compassion, thinking about others, giving them support and strength for holding up to the circumstances beyond our imaginations. In my mind, God still exists and there are reasons for everything that happens. And he made man to be superior above the animals, so he can take care of them and all of nature and the oceans and sky around him. For on the seventh day, he was able to rest; to see that everything was good!

Carol Kappes 2011
(Written in my opinion, **TO ALL NATIONS**.
With religion and language variances in mind.)
In Dedication to RA Inspired by networking

Warfare Takes a Toll On Nations-
It Must Be Stopped!

Conflicts—Talk about the conflict, find the solution,
        make a change. Every Nation
        Must be accountable--Make a compromise and
        stick to it—and very soon!

Economy—Weakens the system of government and society.
        Money is not moving
        And distribution of produce and goods limited and in
        chaotic state.

People—They often wonder, what is happening?
        When will it end? How can a
        Person live in peace with tension? Are they confused,
        angry, and bitter?

Destruction—It was built and destroyed in seconds.
        Progress and development has
        Been stopped and delayed. Lives lost and tremendous pain
        once again.

Emotions—Are the people immune to violence?
        Is it a lifestyle for them?
        Does their behavior coincide with the war's effects? Think
        on this!

Protection—Are the nation's police, armed forces protecting
        the citizens? Do they target
        The groups that cause violence as terrorists, gangs, crime &
        hate groups?

Civilized—Are we becoming strong, educated and lawful
        abiding citizens? Or is the
        Damages done to our character, our responsibilities and
        our conscience?

Atmosphere—Nuclear particles leaking in the air.
        What will it do to the human
        Body and our future generations? Will it cause fear and
        birth defects?

Weaponry—Is this a cause of power or hatred?
        Whatever the use; why cause bloodshed
        To human life? Its use was for hunting and protection of
        citizen's well-being.

Carol Kappes 2011
Dedicated to RS
Inspired from networking for
Changes in the Middle East-
And all Nations Accountable
For peace of conflicts

If All I Ask. . .

If all I ask is fairness
For all the people in this world
What would it be?

It would be for your happiness
It would be for your love
It would be for your future
It would be for your welfare

If all I ask is kindness
For all the people in this world
What would it be?

It would be for your care
It would be for your family
It would be for your society
It would be for your emotions

If all I ask is rightness
For all the people in this world
What would it be?

It would be for your safety
It would be for your strength
It would be for your freedom
It would be for your ability

If all I ask is justness
For all the people in this world
What would it be?

It would be for your peace
It would be for your progress
It would be for your mind
It would be for your soul

Carol Kappes 2012
Inspired for a better world
Current events of Israel/Gaza conflict

I Will Be Back

I will be back in a few weeks'
Somehow the last verse seemed
To have made my heart weak!

I think of all the problems
That could be solved, and why
We aren't taking a stand.

The pursuit of happiness, love,
And peace should be given to ALL
In every corner of the world!

Just as it was designed to be!

Carol Kappes 2011

How Can We Change the World?

Clean it up
Redecorate it
Improve ourselves
Think differently
Let happiness in
Change our thoughts
Keep working
Be more neighborly
Work in unity
Willing to share
Be more helpful
Be more giving
Be more sharing
Show empathy
Try understanding
Be able to reason
Be more loving
Show more kindness
Be thankful
Appreciate more

It's a world in progress!

Carol Kappes 2012

Bloodshed In the Middle East

This has been going on for 40 years or so
I was a young child listening to the news
I grew up in West. This is still going on.
Where is the strong leadership and faith?
We all are humans; with intelligent minds.

I grew up believing in a peaceful world
Believing in caring for one another
Believing in helping each other
Believing in being neighborly
Believing in doing good; not evil.

I wish I could understand your thinking
What it is that carries in your thoughts?
I would not want generations to continue
In witnessing bloodshed into the future.
What is left for these people's welfare?

If this were me; I'd become so sad and weary
I couldn't have that smile on my face.
I would not see the happiness or even feel it
I would wonder what kind of world we live in.
I would be restless and agitated by what I see.

In order to stop this; there has to be a turnaround.
A justice and dignity must prevail and win.
An extreme need of education and reform
A desire of love and kindness for everyone
And a lasting hope of our life in the world.

Carol Kappes 2012
Inspired of Syria crisis

Protest

Use your voice and concern
Show respect while there
Tell and report what's wrong.

Use guidance in your actions
Never use force or violence
Find your reason to protest.

Your hurts are being heard
Mention where it is wronged
Emotions become overdriven.

Chaos develops when angry
Hell breaks loose wildly as
Understanding has been lost.

Carol Kappes 2012
Inspired by world events
Respect religion and cultures

Global

It's a New Beginning For:

A Birth.............The process of bringing forth an offspring or any beginning of an existence.

An Era............A beginning of time marked by an event or a notation of a given date during a distinctive period.

A Choice.........An opportunity to choose and make a careful selection that is preferred. Ones' destiny begins to emerge.

A Generation......A group in ten year increments that are near same age, have similar ideas, problems and attitudes in the nation.

A Global Society...A worldwide, universal celestial globe where the operating of information is using computer commands in single steps. Involving understanding of cultures, personalities, and relations of humankind.

A Lifetime.........A duration in the life committing to work, finding purpose/meaning for existence, and obtaining knowledge, wisdom, and understanding.

A Death.............A moment in time when it's an ending of an existence. The burial takes place in silence.

It's the world continuously moving!

Carol Kappes 2011
Inspired by co-networker

It's a Global Society

And I'm in it; you're in it-

We connect
We network
We get ideas
We receive thoughts
We share information
We read
We laugh.

We seem there, don't we?
Like we're face to face,
Except it's on live video cam...

Interacting
Socializing
Communicating
Entertaining
Chatting
To one another.

How cool is that!

Carol Kappes 2012
Inspired of social networking

Across the Ocean-

I had felt your love
I had felt your culture
I had felt your knowledge
I had felt your awareness
I had felt your music
I had felt your religion
I had felt your emotions
I had felt your lifestyle
I had felt your people
I had felt your language
I had felt your nature
I had felt your friendship
I had felt your desires
I had felt your laughter
I had felt your connection
I had felt your presence
I had felt your happiness

Carol Kappes 2011
Inspired by e-mails
And instant messages
From networking
Dedicated to MH

It Is YOU

YOU left such an impression on me,
that I can't get you out of my mind!

Only YOU can make things happen.

YOU make my life shine bright.

It was YOU who taught me to love.

It's a joy when I see YOU.

I love YOU!

Carol Kappes 2011
Inspired by networking friends

A Good Morning

Good morning
> Sweet sunshine
>> Have a great day!!
N super hug
> From far away!!!

Secret networker (written verse)
Carol Kappes (written title)
In collaboration 2012

I Long For You. . .

I long to feel your touch
　　　To feel your love
　　　　　To feel you.

I long to see your eyes
　　　To see your gaze
　　　　　To see you.

I long to kiss your lips
　　　To kiss your desire
　　　　　To kiss you.

I long to smell your hair
　　　To smell your perfume
　　　　　To smell you.

I long to hear your voice
　　　To hear your breath
　　　　　To hear you.

Carol Kappes 2012
Inspired of online dating

You're On My Mind

Here I am lying awake in bed,
Thinking of things you've often said.
It's been sometime since we've kept in touch
And I realize just how I miss you so much.

Hope you enjoy yourself and have a great time
For life is to be enjoyed while in your prime.
Although I think of you many miles away;
Will there be a time when you might stay?

Carol Kappes 1985
Revised last line 2012

My First Year At Blogging

I hope that I have touched your heart
I hope that I have brightened your life
I hope that I have given you direction
I hope that I have given you happiness
I hope that I have opened your future
I hope that I have given you ideas
I hope that I have helped in any way
I hope that I have counseled you
I hope that I have shown you kindness
I hope that I have given you faith
I hope that I have lifted your pain
I hope that I have shown you courage
I hope that I have lifted your spirits
I hope that I have encouraged your day
I hope that I have defined real love
I hope that I have reached out to you
I hope that I have voiced your concerns
I hope that I have delivered a message
I hope that I have connected with you
I hope that I have strengthened you

Carol Kappes 2011
An Author of Verse
Carol's Corner
Started on Jan. 12, 2011

My 2nd Year Of Blogging

I've shared my lifestyle; along with knowing yours
I've shared my religion; as to understand yours
I've shared my music; along with hearing yours
I've shared my childhood; as to simple as yours
I've shared my wisdom; along with knowledge of yours
I've shared my health; as to improve yours
I've shared my language; along with translating yours
I've shared my happiness; as to reciprocate yours
I've shared my pictures; along with seeing yours
I've shared my thoughts; as to educate yours
I've shared my ideals; along with interpreting yours

Carol Kappes 2012
An Author of Verse
Carol's Corner
Began January 12, 2011

Dynamite

To Kill?

Who? What? Where? When? Why?
This does not make any sense-
Deliberate taking a human life
Suddenly put to an early death.

Isn't the animal world less vicious?
Do they take away their own species?
Animals kill so they can survive
It's a matter of life or death for them.

But us humans taking our own kind
For unlawful, selfish, and political reasons?
Causing bloodshed within our people is
Becoming a national crisis within humanity.

Carol Kappes 2011
Collaborated thoughts
Inspired of bombing, threats, shooting
From actual events in nations

Harsh

Words

Criticism

Treatment

Weather

Sentence

Discipline

Beating

Carol Kappes 2013
Inspired of the harmful
Effects to another person

It's a Wake-up Call

When the alarm clock rings
When a nurse on duty comes in
When the doctor reports a disease
When an accident has occurred
When family, friend, or relative dies
When your child became lost
When counting the months to live
When a disaster has struck
When an intruder breaks in
When someone is kidnapped
When bitten by a strange animal
When struck by lightning
When terrorists attack a nation
When someone is killed or shot

Carol Kappes 2012
Inspired to "Be on guard"

I Faced the Devil. . .

He breaks your heart
He diseases your mind
He tears you apart
He corrals you in
He establishes your body
He stunts your growth
He messes your thoughts
He wants your sinfulness
He hates your wisdom
He leads you astray
He stresses your identity
He disables your dignity
He destroys your emotions
He defaces your image
He endangers your psyche
He corrupts your beauty
He plays you wrong
He took your advantage
He condemns your obedience
He weakens your strength
He deadens your feelings
He chokes your breath
He controls your tongue
He cheats your behavior
He denies your trust
He crashes your faith
He curses your job

He depletes your finances
He vandalizes your progress
He rebukes your conduct
He lowers your standards
He parasites your family
He robs your worth
He despises your looks
He spoils your manners
He trashes your personality
He envelopes your kindness
He cusses your character
He quenches your spirit
He weakens your discipline
He threatens your self-esteem
He scorns your righteousness
He steals your love
He tempts your soul
He smothers your words
He deceives morality

Carol Kappes 2012
Inspired of true distaste,
Aversion, hate, loathe

Head-On

Something occurred today that
Made me very distraught and sad.
Many tears flowed down my face.

Sometimes life throws you one like a
Head-on collision--that you don't know
Whether you'll survive it or not.

Carol Kappes 2012
Inspired by
Life's hardships

Unforeseen Conditions

And how has your year
Been coming along so far?

I tell you, mine definitely is
Unlike any other years…
Maybe taking a nosedive?

Unforeseen conditions came
By like those storms do.

Better get that plane back
To altitude before it gets
Even WORSE!

Carol Kappes 2013
Inspired of incidents that happen

Genocide/Infanticide/Femicide

The taking of a life

An act of human violence

Destruction of humanity

Acting out of hatred

Immoral thoughts manifested

Hostility towards a person

Suffering is evident

Inflicting pain and wounds

Casualties caused by evil

Carol Kappes 2013

Evil

Evil can be seen in the eyes
Evil can be heard in the anger
Evil can be voiced in the words
Evil can be felt in the push
Evil can be bullying in the student
Evil can be neglect in the family
Evil can be disrespect in relations
Evil can be killing in peoples' lives
Evil can be damage in the mind
Evil can be lies in the statement
Evil can be fraud in the document
Evil can be stealing in the merchandise
Evil can be forgotten in the homeless
Evil can be disloyal in the partnership
Evil can be abuse in the women
Evil can be abortion in the fetus
Evil can be rape in the victim
Evil can be hatred in the people
Evil can be pain in the society
Evil can be harassment in the employee
Evil can be lies in the conversation
Evil can be gossip in the rumor
Evil can be alcohol/drugs in the driver
Evil can be corrupt in the government
Evil can be terrorist in the country
Evil can be threaten in the person
Evil can be violence in the weapon

Evil can be addiction in the brain
Evil can be harmful in the actions
Evil can be immoral in the thoughts
Evil can be cheating in the test
Evil can be betrayal in the spouse
Evil can be disgrace in the reputation
Evil can be control in the marriage
Evil can be affair in the relationship
Evil can be deny in the trust
Evil can be blame in others
Evil can be greed in the money
Evil can be dishonest in the love
Evil can be torture in the prisoner
Evil can be war in the nation

Carol Kappes 2011

A Beating (Brutality)

Does this give you a "natural high?"
Is this how you get "power?"
Do you like to "humiliate" others?
Do you like to see "suffering?"
Why do you "laugh" about it?
Do you like to "hurt" others?

What did you "gain" from it?
What "circumstances" lead to it?
What "feelings" do you have from it?
What "apologies" or "guilt" is there?
What "dignity" is there in you?
What "motivates" you to do this?

Think… before you react!

Carol Kappes 2013
Dedicated to BB
Inspired of Aggression, Bullies

Comfort

A Cup Of Coffee Or Tea?

It sure is chilly this morning--
What would you like to drink?
I want to share that cup with you!

We can talk about the weather
Or what's happening in the news.
How is your career going for you?
Or how is your family doing?

We can talk about the schools
Or what's happening to youth.
How is your health been for you?
Or how is life treating you?

It sure was a pleasant morning--
What would you have thought?
I'm glad to share that cup with you!

Carol Kappes 2011
Inspired by networking

A Rainbow Of Joy

Soon may that rainbow shine
Many colors for your future!

May it be bright with multi-facets
Like jewelry that sparkles to eternity.

Hope that your daughter/son comes
Through with mystical signs of life.

And splendid rain that pours
Buckets of joy into your heart.

Carol Kappes 2012
Inspired of full recovery
For someone special

Speedy Recovery

May God give you courage,
Strength and His love
For your speedy recovery!

He will take care of you
If you can't...

Carol Kappes 2012
To a special friend
Dedicated to DC

You Speak From the Heart. . .

When you smile

When you cry

When you listen

When you ask

When you pray

When you forgive

When you help

When you share

When you care

When you give

When you love

Carol Kappes 2012
Inspired of grace

A Sip Of Wine

I just took that sip
Of Italian red wine
From a beautiful glass.

My, how tasteful it
Was on my palate today;
It quenched my thirst.

It gives me a joy after
A long day's hard work;
Perfect for the evening.

Makes the day complete
When you share it with
The one you truly love!

Carol Kappes 9/2011
Inspired on vacation

What Is Sweet?

It can be candy

It can be a baby/child

It can be your beloved

It can be a moment

It can be something you eat

It can be something you drink

It can be a surprise

It can be your happiness

It can be a fragrance

It can be something you said

It can be something you hear

It can be your pet

It can be a compliment

It can be in a greeting

It can be your love

Carol Kappes 2012

We Say Blessed In. . .

God bless you

I feel blessed

A blessed event

Count your blessings

A blessed life

Stay blessed

Bless our home

Blessing of a meal

Blessed by God

Keep it nearby!

Carol Kappes 2011

Tranquility

A warm, luxurious bath
A sound of water trickles
A room to relax yourself
A snuggle of a cozy blanket
A playing of soft music
An instrumental sound
A scene of nature's beauty
An interesting landmark
A snowflake falling down
An ocean's wave coming in
A beach of whitened sand
A bouquet of flowers
A blue, clouded sky
A redwood tall and strong
A glimpse of native animals
A rainbow after the rain
A beverage of warmth
A delicious, tasty treat
A moment of silence
A midday summer nap
A candle displays a light
A love so honest and true

A peace within the mind

A language for the soul

A quietness all around

A moment of happiness

A love, strong and gentle

A passionate embrace

An intimacy of a couple

A baby in mothers' arms

A prayer of thankfulness

Carol Kappes 2013

Blue Nun Wine

We sure enjoy the taste of Blue Nun wine
As we sit here to dine.
With laughter all around
And snow upon the ground
Everything is wonderful and fine!

Carol Kappes 1986
Verse for Blue Nun wine offer

As My Friend

My heart made you
As my friend-
I'll remember you
To the very end!

Emotions of love
Given to me
Fits like a glove
As you can see.

Memories come often
As I think of you
Brings me back when,
You were so true.

Carol Kappes 2011

I Wish I Could...

Sit at a bistro table with you
Have that red glass of wine;
Enjoying the most perfect meal

With the soft music playing
As I make conversation with you
In the darkness of the night.

If only dreams were to be true-
I'd like to spend time with you.

Carol Kappes 2011
Inspired by friends

Two Peas In a Pod

Yes, we are two peas in a pod
Till harvest comes in the fall.
Then what will happen to us?

Will we remain together or
Separate; and never see or
Be with one another again?

Only the seconds, minutes,
Hours, days, weeks, months,
And years will determine this.

Carol Kappes 2012
Inspired of love

Love

Neighborly love

Friendship love

Companionship love

Elderly love

Young love

Family love

Gentle love

Mutual love

Respectful love

Emotional love

Passionate love

Sexual love

Romantic love

Divine love

Many forms of love!

Carol Kappes 2012

My Dogs Miss Me

Now that I am away
My dogs miss me.
To this very day
I also miss thee.

They were my comfort
In life's many trials.
And when I use to hurt
They brought me smiles.

To their very end
I'll take care of them.
I was glad to attend
As they were my friend!

Carol Kappes 2011
Inspired by pets

Home

Through the Years

Today we became joined together
To share our dreams, our thoughts,
          And our love.

As we travel on throughout life's pathways,
We'll always be needing the help from
          God above.

And as the years pass swiftly on by us,
We'll know that it all began with our
          True and constant love.

Carol Kappes 1986

To Have and To Hold

I guess I couldn't live
Anymore without
Your love

You have made me
Very happy in
My life

I thought about you
A lot since the day
I met you

You were my light
When days seemed
So dark

I knew my love
Would always be
With you

You make me smile
When times get
Really tough

I will always cherish
Your love forever
Till I die

Carol Kappes 2012
Inspired of engagement
And marriage

Being Together

Here we are together at last;
Those days of absence are in the past.

We can begin our journey now,
Since we've taken our final vow.

Where we go or what we have become;
Adds up to our life in one big sum.

And the accomplishments that we've made
Will stay with us and never fade.

Carol Kappes 1986

Your Love

Oh, honey! You are so sweet to me,
It's just the way I want it to be.

Your happy face and loving touch,
Makes me want you so very much.

Continue this always year after year,
And you'll see that I'll always be near!

Carol Kappes 1986

Like-Minded

We see things similar
We want trust together
We show same interests
We like familiar things
We involve each other
We take things in stride
We work out differences
We converse to each other
We share and enjoy fun
We find some excitement
We agree mutually
We don't take sides
We confess to faults
We show that we care
We love one another
We evolve together
We cry with each other
We work out difficulties
We share the load of tasks
We lift each other's spirit
We comfort one another

Carol Kappes 2011

Please Take Care Of Me

In the good days and the bad days,
With the great times and the difficult times.

When things are well and when they're not
Or when we feel too sick to carry on.

Sometimes I need a shoulder to lean on
When trouble comes my way and yours.

Lots of love will keep us strong but at
Some point it could make a wrong-

So talk with me and stand beside me,
Through all the days within our life.

For when the final curtain has arrived-
We knew in our death, we would part.

Carol Kappes 2011
Inspired for lasting love

Marriage Partners Need. . .

I need love and you need love
I need a smile and you need a smile
I need a kiss and you need a kiss
I need respect and you need respect
I need honesty and you need honesty
I need support and you need support
I need prayer and you need prayer
I need forgiveness and you need forgiveness
I need a compliment and you need a compliment
I need happiness and you need happiness
I need trust and you need trust
I need care and you need care
I need kindness and you need kindness
I need loyalty and you need loyalty
I need to talk and you need to talk
I need to listen and you need to listen
I need to share and you need to share
I need a hug and you need a hug
I need pleasure and you need pleasure
I need closeness and you need closeness
I need devotion and you need devotion
I need laughter and you need laughter
I need intimacy and you need intimacy
I need fulfillment and you need fulfillment
I need commitment and you need commitment

Carol Kappes 2011
In collaboration
Dedicated to MI

Kiss Me Goodbye

When you leave for work
And kiss me goodbye,
You leave with me your
Scent of cologne that still
Lingers on my lips and face.

It stays there for at least an
Hour, and I still think about
You. I think about the night
We shared, the laughter we
Had, and the fun we created.

And I love you so much…

Carol Kappes 2013
Dedicated to CA-CM
Inspired of relationships

The Married Life

Marriage is like a roller coaster-
It has its ups and downs!
Moving along with love and laughter
Then sometimes tears and frowns.

Coasting along with so much speed
One tends to grip on so tight
And hoping it will eventually lead
Them safely to the ground in sight.

Tensions rise and feelings come out
At various parts of the ride
But when it stops, without a doubt
One is filled with joy inside!

Carol Kappes 1987

An Evergreen Marriage

Maybe we should think of marriage
Like the evergreen tree.

Decorate it each year with faith,
Hope, peace, love, and trust.

Be creative and keep it fresh, give
It water, and it should take root and
Continue to grow through the years.

It will weather the storm a few times
During the year; but with nurture,
It will gain continued strength.

Carol Kappes 2013
In collaboration
Dedicated to SK
Inspired of a faith-filled,
Loving marriage

It's Night and I Miss You

Sometimes as I lie in bed
I clasp both hands together.

Your hand will be in mine,
As I think about you now.

It has a special feeling as
If you're lying next to me.

This helps my mind knowing
Your love is here with me.

This warms my heart till I
Fall asleep into the late night.

I said a little prayer for safety;
The day you travel back to me.

Carol Kappes 2011
Inspired of loved one away

Don't Let Your Love Die-

Please stay married!
Keep the love alive
Devote to one another
Still do all the fun things
Keep going out on dates
Show respect and love
Pay attention all the time
Relieve your stress together
Shower thoughts of love
Care deeply for each other
Listen to one another
Spread your devotion
Pray for happiness and peace
Love your children equally
Keep the family in unity
Cry out problems together
Don't take each other for granted
Remember your first dates
Listen to your favorite songs
Continue through the years
Look back to the day you met
Stay connected together
Remember your marriage vows
Remember your ceremony
Make it last till death do you part

Carol Kappes 2011

Lovemaking

Desire and kissing
Loving and caressing
Indulging and inviting
Exciting and romancing
Embracing and fondling
Sensual and passionate
Intercourse and ecstasy

Carol Kappes 2013
Inspired of courtship/marriage
Dedicated to SA

Life

On this beautiful day
As the children go out to play
I bow my head to pray—

That into the near future
They will see a joyful picture
And not be fallen by a lure.

From up above they will be blessed
Given peace, strength; and not be stressed
As life becomes fully dressed.

On this beautiful day
I bow my head to pray—
As my children went out to play.

Carol Kappes 2003

Pets

I have a pet, inside my home-
A friend to me when I'm alone.

The time spent watching it moving about
Brings a joy to me without a doubt.

I call her "Chubs," a golden hamster
With tiny eyes, feet, and shaggy fur.

Pets certainly are a man's best friend-
And we'll love them to their very end!

Carol Kappes 1987
Inspired of companionship
With domestic animals

Health

Take Care Of Your Teeth-

You use them every day to eat
They help you pronounce words
They add depth to your cheeks
They are part of your identity
Brush two times a day and floss
Rinse with proper mouthwash
See your dentist once/ twice a year
Early detection means lower costs
Prevention of cavities and loss of teeth
Maintains overall health and looks

Carol Kappes 2011
Licensed dental assistant career

Balm Your Lips

It's so important to keep
Them subtle and pretty.

Be it summer time
From hot, scorching sun

Be it winter time
From dry, warm heat

You don't want to end up
With dry, cracked lips!

Always keep them moist

Carol Kappes 2011

Slim Down, Please!
(Carol's Health Plan)

Slim down your weight for yourself and others

Take a multi-vitamin each and every day

Eat much smaller meals (very small portion size)

Eat all food groups in moderation and not excess

Limit salad dressings, high calorie snacks, etc

Limit your sweets, limited alcoholic and sugar drinks

When you find yourself hungry; eat fruit, drink water!

Not like plain water? Add lemon or lime juice to taste

Walk daily at morning, lunch, and/or evening

Do push-ups, lift arm weights, leg lifts, and cardio

You've noticed you have more energy and stamina

You weighed yourself and lost 5 pounds this week!

You're feeling like a whole new person once again

You've measured into more fashionable clothes now

You've seen emotional habits lessen or disappear

Continue and retain your new ideals of your weight

Now thank yourself for a healthy body and outlook!

Carol Kappes 2012
Inspired of healthy body,
Outlook, and lifestyle

Our Body Made Into Three Parts:

PHYSICAL-We must nourish our body with food, drink, and essential multi-vitamins. Eat many varieties of meals and drink in moderation. Target on meats, grains, vegetables and fruit. And don't forget to treat yourself with a dessert! Keep yourself physically fit and well. Remember to move that body! It is designed to walk and run and stay in activities. Sitting and sleeping is done too; we all need a little rest. We are to take great care of that body by no overuse of drugs and/or alcohol. Use these items sparingly to stay healthy. Don't deny yourself. If others see you need help, listen to them. They care and love you!

MENTAL- We must see things clearly with the capacity of our mind. Look and listen; watch in interest of the world around you. Don't only look into yourself. There are others all around so learn about feelings and emotions. Learn about what's good and bad, and seek to find your values. As you study and observe through personal growth, look into your strengths and interests; rather than what everyone is doing. If one jumps over the cliff, will you follow? "No." So remember to find your own talents. This will carry you into your choice of college, career, and employment.

SPIRITUAL-We must know the reason we're here. We were born for a life to live. Take an interest in finding out why. As children we wanted to explore-now we can again. Read the WORD and learn an understanding of your faith. Love one another as He has loved you. Love your neighbor as yourself. Keep that feeling of love in your heart! Don't push it away. If it is pushed away, how will you get it back? It could take a long time through your journey. An on-going intimate relationship with Him through active meditation and prayers, will give you the peace and understanding to your life.

Use them all wisely

Carol Kappes 2011
Inspired of living a full life
In good health

Love Yourself to Love Others

Love your body...

> Nourish it with the right foods
> Bathe and clean it with soaps
> Take care of it with lotions
> and skin products
> Groom it with combs, brushes,
> and razors
> Beautify it with make-up, style,
> and fashion
> Personalize it with diet, exercise,
> and weight control
> Educate it with continuous learning
> Calm it with meditation and prayer

When you do this...

> It increases self-help
> It increases self-awareness
> It increases self-esteem
> It increases self-motivation
> It increases self-confidence
> It increases self-control
> It increases self-development
> It increases self-discovery

And you become more acceptable to others!

Carol Kappes 2012
Inspired to become more independent
And loving towards others

I Misplaced My Eye Glasses, Keys. . .

You hear this often as we age
Make a note of this right now.

From now on, find a good location
Where you will always place them.

Designate two areas in your home
Where you keep them, when not in use.

You don't ever want the same excuse
Has anyone seen my _____ yet?

Because we all know that it was YOU
Who forgot now where you left them!

Carol Kappes 2011
Inspired by the Aging Mind
Forgetfulness, Dementia,
And Alzheimer's Disease

Your Mind

Don't lose it
Don't disorder it
Don't prison it
Don't abuse it
Don't hinder it
Don't waste it
Don't abandon it
Don't hunger it
Don't dirty it
Don't anger it
Don't addict it
Don't poison it
Don't sicken it
Don't neglect it
Don't threaten it
Don't exhaust it
Don't injure it
Don't destroy it
Don't weaken it
Don't ignore it

Keep it safe!

Carol Kappes 2012
Inspired of a healthy mind

What Makes Your Life Cloudy?

Is it that you aren't busy enough?
Maybe you need to work on something?

Find an interest that you can do.
Start small and work up from there.

Is it that you want to improve yourself?
Maybe you need a style that's you?

Find the clothes and products to enhance.
Start personalizing yourself well.

Is it that you want some character?
Try honesty, trust, and reputation.

Find the traits, status, and morals in you.
Develop these qualities to reach it.

Is it that you rely on others?
Try to volunteer for something.

Find the act of helping instead.
Start seeing yourself with strength.

Is it that you don't understand?
Maybe you need advice from others.

Find someone to answer your question.
Start entries to your bank of knowledge.

Is it that you are in the wrong crowd?
Maybe you need different new friends.

Find people that are similar to you.
Start promoting yourself higher.

Is it that you are anxious or nervous?
Maybe you need more confidence.

Find someone with encouragement to help.
Develop abilities within yourself.

Is it that you don't feel well?
Try walking and being outdoors, too.

Find the sun and atmosphere.
Develop healthy eating and lifestyle skills.

Is it that you feel so sad right now?
Try talking it out to someone.

Find a support group or person.
Start seeing the sun thru others view.

Bring back the sunshine soon!

Carol Kappes 2011
Inspired by feelings
That people have.

I Want a New Life

It has become stale.
It is lacking in spirit.
It seems like it died.

Shall I buy a new life?
Where can I order it from?
Will it be better?
How can I improve it?

Maybe it needs a new outlook?
Maybe it requires more energy?
Maybe it needs some activity?

Just revive it with new ideas,
Thoughts, and adventures!

Carol Kappes 2012
Dedicated to JL

Never Hold a Grudge...

It sets you back

It controls you

It stays within you

It is useless to keep

It can weaken you

It has no strength

It takes up space

It brings in more

It consumes you

It can destroy you

Learn why it happens!

Carol Kappes 2012
Inspired from people who
Resents someone/thing

My Heart Surgery

I just recently came out of my heart surgery
And made it back into the life I've known.

I've kept a positive attitude that helped me make it through
To see yet the joys and wonders of my life as the days continue.

I am still needed here on this earth
To use my talents and become more wise.

Carol Kappes 1986

Warmth

Touch

I'm touched by your words/
Your touch is inviting;
Feel the softness of touch.

I'm touched by your thoughts/
Your touch is thrilling;
Feel the magic of touch.

I'm touched by your empathy/
Your touch is astounding;
Feel the wonder of touch.

I'm touched by your kindness/
Your touch is amazing;
Feel the happiness of touch.

I'm touched by your smile/
Your touch is exciting;
Feel the passion of touch.

I'm touched by your joy/
Your touch is pleasuring;
Feel the love of touch.

Carol Kappes 2011
Inspired by the emotional aspect of
Touch and the sense of touch

You're Like a Puppy

I love it...

When you greet me at the door
When you offer your hand
When you get overly excited
When you have a charming face
When you indulge in delicate treats
When you beg me to come

I hate it...

When you whimper too much
When you bark so loudly
When you lost the need to wait
When you attacked for no reason
When you chew down your friends
When you dig into things

Carol Kappes 2013
Dedicated to MV

A Porcelain Doll

You are so special and beautiful

You are so detailed and attractive

You are so delicate and fragile

You are so exquisite and spotless

You are so charming and mine!

Carol Kappes 2012
Inspired from networking
Dedicated to MAS

Love Notes To You

Please be there for me-as I will for you
Stay happy for me and you
Take some of my sunshine; and brighten your day with it
Do something with me today
We're on this road together
You bring excitement to my life
Your love flows deep within my heart
Stay with me tonight
You give me lots of pleasure
I'll always remember this day
Keep your thoughts beside me
Send me your love soon; I'm missing you
I need you to hold me
In your heart, you know that I will always love you, want
you, and need you for comfort
We're oceans apart, e-mail me
Nothing in this world will tear us apart
Please take care of me
Your love is important to me
Text me when you get the chance
You will always be in my mind
You are very special to me
Your eyes show true love
You take my breath away
Fate has brought us together
I want to love you tonight

Carol Kappes 2011

A Kiss For You:

To love you
　　　To honor you
　　　　　To respect you

When I leave
　　　When I'm away
　　　　　When I'm back

To desire you
　　　To relish you
　　　　　To pleasure you

In good times
　　　In happy times
　　　　　In sad times

With greetings
　　　With family members
　　　　　With goodbyes

Carol Kappes 2012

A Heart Of. . .

Gold............Precious, loving, beautiful

Diamond......Brilliant, shiny, pure

Steel............Strong, strength, powerful

Copper.........Warmth, smooth, natural

Magnet........Attraction, committed, bond

Gem............Valuable, colorful, perfect

Stone..........Cold, unrefined, hard

Clay............ Sticky, porous, dry

Coal............Combustible, dull, black

Dirt............Loose, filthy, organic

Sand...........Infinite, grain, tiny

Carol Kappes 2012
Dedicated to NC

A Real Gem!

Sometimes in life
Very few people can
Make a place in ur heart

And u r damm sure
1 of them..a real gem...
Thank you.

Carol Kappes (Written Title)
Social Networker (Written Verse)
Dedicated to AS
In collaboration 2013

Capture the Moment

You look younger than me
You feel younger than me
You are younger than me
If we were at the same place,
I would have asked you out for a dinner!

Social networker (written verse)
Carol Kappes (written title)
Dedicated to MO
In collaboration Jan. 2013

Every Time You Leave, I Miss . . .

Your smile
Your embrace
Your kiss

Your strength
Your love
Your passion

Your presence
Your voice
Your affection

Your words
Your laughter
Your gentleness

I can't wait to see you again!

Carol Kappes 2011

Fruits and Vegs Of You

You are as tart as an apple
You are as lovely as a peach
You are as bright as a cherry
You are as bold as a blackberry
You are as sweet as a kiwi
You are as sour as a grapefruit
You are as superior as a strawberry
You are as tangy as an orange
You are as mellow as a cantaloupe
You are as blush as a watermelon
You are as tangible as a plum
You are as rough as a pineapple
You are as smooth as a banana
You are as sunny as a lemon
You are as late as a date
You are as seedy as a raspberry
You are as mild as a tangerine
You are as fine as a lime
You are as bitter as a grape
You are as blue as a blueberry
You are as thick as an apricot
You are as mature as a cranberry
You are as shaped as a pear
You are as juicy as a mango
You are as savor as a papaya
You are as delicate as an avocado
You are as tasty as a pomegranate

You are as firm as rhubarb
You are as cool as a cucumber
You are as ornery as a corn
You are as starchy as a potato
You are as sure as a pumpkin
You are as dark as an eggplant
You are as ripe as a tomato
You are as red as a beet
You are as crisp as celery
You are as smitten as a radish
You are as suppress as a squash
You are as perky as spinach
You are as hard as a carrot
You are as sharp as an onion
You are as best as lettuce
You are as loose as cabbage
You are as green as peas
You are as mean as beans
You are as peppy as green pepper
You are as boast as a mushroom
You are as little as a gourd

Carol Kappes 2012

DEFINE LOVE.
What Is the Power Of LOVE?

Love is the warm embrace, the passionate kiss, the touch of your hair, the scent of perfume, and the making of LOVE!

Love is the mother's bond, the infant cuddled, the proud father, the joyful moment, and the blessing from ABOVE!

Love is the helping hand, the food prepared, the medicines given, the shelter found, and the people COMFORTED!

Love is the guiding light, the chosen path, the righteous one, the true believers, and the way to HEAVEN!

Carol Kappes 2011
Inspired of love created

You Are Magnetized

By my eyes

By my lips

By my smile

By my hair

By my kiss

By my embrace

By my touch

By my words

By my charm

By my grace

By my love

By my energy

By my spirit

By my desire

By my passion

Carol Kappes 2011

What Is a Soulmate?

Someone that thinks similar to you
Someone that talks easily with you
Someone that displays understanding
Someone that has same qualities
Someone that displays connectedness
Someone that their visions coincide
Someone that their emotions equal
Someone that conveys great affection
Someone that devotes in deep love
Someone that shows constant loyalty

Carol Kappes 2011

Heartache

Why Does He Blame Me?

I'm living in the life of hate
He feels as though it's my fault
He lives a self-centered life
When he's married to a wife.

She feels so sad a lot of times
Thinking there will be a turn-around
A miracle to help things out
But this can't seem to; no doubt.

It came to pass with this mess
Conflicts became strong with anger
No way can I continue on with this
I have to move away for some bliss.

Living with someone who craves
His drink of alcohol to get his high
Was never pleasant anymore so
He said it was time for me to go.

When he should blame himself!

Carol Kappes 2011
Inspiration due to:
Drug/Alcohol Abuse
Domestic violence
Marriage Dissolution

Handle With Love

Relationships resemble a rubber band;
They stretch in ways we don't understand!

At times they're strong and reliable,
Sometimes they're weak and very pliable.

When they break, we try to mend them;
As a tailor would finish a hem.

When they are no longer in use,
We always find an excuse.

Always handle each one with proper care;
So they remain firm, avoiding a tear!

Carol Kappes 1986

Divorce Aftermath

Receiving the Dissolution of Marriage
Feeling the emotional grief of rejection
Mental anguish escapes the numbed mind
Mend from the support and advice given
The suffering and the pain becomes less
Your strength is gained as an individual
Looking for another place to live
Division of personal property and possessions
Judgment and Decree finalized
Moving out and separating family
Thoughts come across to your children's life
God happens to be there with you now
Beginning to feel whole and loved again
Deleting from the mind memories from the past
Beginning to feel love and happiness again
Knowing that many others still care for you
Realize that life does go on for you to enjoy
Your mind once again shows courage to begin

Carol Kappes 2012
Inspired of the Divorce
Emotional effects

Problems

Should we try to sweep them under the rug?
I don't think so; that would make you a coward.

Should we do something about it?
I would definitely give it a try.

Should we give it our best thought?
I would certainly do so, it's worth it.

Should we discuss how to handle it?
I want to know the best and easiest way.

Should we both work together at it?
I would want us both to solve it together.

Should we be able to fix it for good?
I would think so, till the next one shows up!

Carol Kappes 2011

Greed

You have become very selfish
Only think of your own needs
You do not want to share
Think you're better than others
Shows signs of disrespect
Do not live a Godly life
You want to fulfill your desires
You feast while others suffer
Decisions based on your choices
An effect that you want more
Your ego has become self-centered

Carol Kappes 2012
Inspired of Greed

Short Fuse

Men are known for this--a short fuse

Does it have to do with ego or power?
Does it have to do with anger or hatred?
Does it have to do with impatience?
Does it have to do with irresponsibility?
Does it have to do with reasoning skills?
Does it have to do with not listening?
Does it have to do with misunderstanding?
Does it have to do with meanness or bullying?
Does it have to do with poor communication?
Does it have to do with lack of knowledge?

Please respect women and children

Carol Kappes 2012
Inspired from networking

You Say Nagging Wife?

Maybe she wants your help?
Maybe she needs things fixed?
Maybe she wants an errand done?
Maybe her needs are not met?
Maybe you don't notice her?
Maybe you put things off?
Maybe you didn't understand her?
Maybe you were angry with her?
Maybe you haven't apologized?
Maybe you aren't organized?
Maybe you haven't been there?
Maybe she needs your attention?
Maybe you weren't compliant with her?
Maybe you aren't grateful of her?
Maybe you don't listen to her?
Maybe you hadn't supported her?
Maybe you didn't agree with her?
Maybe you threatened her?
Maybe you have neglected her?
Maybe you take her for granted?
Maybe she feels overworked?
Maybe you hadn't called her?
Maybe you forget special days?
Maybe she needs companionship?
Maybe she wants your love?
Maybe she feels lonely at times?
Maybe she needs to hear your voice?

A women needs attention!

Carol Kappes 2012
Inspired of neglected love

I Gave You the Chance:

To hear my advice
To better yourself
To get some help
To work things out
To hear my side
To dine with me
To be with me
To accompany me
To make a change
To turn around
To hear my solutions
To talk with me
To reason with me
To understand me
To know my thoughts

But you wouldn't listen!

Carol Kappes 2011
Inspiration of
Relationship difficulties

A Toxic Home

Way too many fumes in the air
Family members are dysfunctional
Living without reason or understanding
Having a negative atmosphere
Creating a massive dust bowl
Can't quite whether the storm
Damage will only get worse
Causing physical and mental pain
Anguish appears in order to cope
Only hope is to get out in safety

Carol Kappes 2013
Inspired of the breakdown
Of family structure

A Mind Break

I want to have a mind break;
Something I just need to take.

It works too hard and I need
The rest...something I deserve!

Love and hate; what a spell-
In this world that God create.

Because of human emotions
We all are at the fault of it.

Carol Kappes 2013
An expressive/emotional writer
Author of Verse
Carol's Corner

Take Control Of Your Habit-

Drinking
Drugs
Gambling
Smoking
Overeating
Tattooing
Nail biting
Procrastinating
Shopping
Womanizing
Lying
Cheating
Swearing
Texting
TV watching
Computing
Video gaming

Before it controls you!

Carol Kappes 2011
Inspired to avoid an
Addiction to the mind

Dogs Remember Me

I had to leave unwanted;
But dogs remember me.

To visit with joint custody
My children whom I love.

When I came back;
Two dogs remember me.

I couldn't even take one
To my place which I rent.

I see them both with joy;
As dogs remember me.

Carol Kappes 2013
Inspired of divorce settlement

Drown

You can drown in water

You can drown in memories

You can drown in substance

You can drown in sorrow

You can drown in self

You can drown in fear

You can drown in sin

You can drown in filth

You can drown in vomit

Carol Kappes 2012
Inspired of hopelessness

Happy

Happiness Is. . .

The air that we breathe
The love that we feel
The rose that we smell
The warmth of the sun
The touch of one's hand
The sound of one's voice
The kindness of one's heart

Carol Kappes 1986

I See Love In Your Eyes. . .

You have that look
You have that gaze
You have that allure
You have that smile
You have that intent
You have that kindness
You have that desire
You have that passion
You have that glow
You have that sparkle
You have that longing
You have that warmth
You have that invite
You have that cue
You have that love

And it sure shows!

Carol Kappes 2012
Dedicated to Su.M

It's Your Birthday

I want the sun's rays
To shine down on you!

You deserve much sunshine
Today for your birthday.

Each moment of each second
Is yours to take on forever.

It couldn't have come down
To someone as nice as you!

Carol Kappes 2012

Only Fair-

How do you feel today
In this warm month of May?
"Just great!" I would say
In the sun's beaming ray.

I noticed it then and there
That you shower me with care.
And it is only to be fair-
We make a splendid pair!

Carol Kappes 1986

She Gave Me the World

Loved me

Admired me

Cared for me

Worried for me

Hoped for me

Prayed for me

Comforted me

Believed for me

Strengthened me

Complimented me

Encouraged me

Thought for me

Defined me

Accepted me

Thanked me

Adored me

Carol Kappes 2012

Sweet As Candy

You are as sweet as candy!
>You have the brightest color
>You have the best of flavor
>You have the pleasant taste
>You have the sugar-coated style
>You have the revealing indulgence

You are mine to thoroughly enjoy!

Carol Kappes 2012
Inspired by a friend

Tender

A special feeling
Just came our way.

Kindness and care
Gentleness and love

Desire and warmth
Pleasure and ecstasy

A tender moment
Was ours today.

Carol Kappes 2012
Inspired of lovemaking

I Attracted Your Heart. . .

Maybe it was my smile?

Maybe it was my eyes?

Maybe it was my hairstyle?

Maybe it was my pleasantness?

Maybe it was my confidence?

Maybe it was my personality?

Maybe it was my intelligence?

Maybe it was my conversation?

Maybe it was my fashion?

Maybe it was my stature?

Maybe it was my beauty?

Carol Kappes 2013
Inspired of Courting, dating

The Beach
(Huntington Beach, CA)

A couple is walking on the beach
The sand in their feet.
The ocean breeze sets the scene
As the ocean waves
Are coming in.

There's laughter and smiles-
There's a hunger of love
Showing in the warm air.

The seagulls swoop down
And he gives her a kiss.
Hair is blowing in the wind
It feels so good tonight!

He holds her so tight
And says, "I love you."
With a sparkle in her eye
She says, "I love you, too."

Carol Kappes 2011
Dedicated to RK

Why Do I Melt
When I See You? It's

Your eyes, your smile, your attraction,
Your charm, your confidence, your strength,
Your character, your manners, your looks,
Your love, your devotion, and your commitment!

I should freeze again, and start all over—

Carol Kappes 2011

You've Touched My Heart. . .

When you've given me a glance

When you've given me that smile

When you've given me your voice

When you've given me that kiss

When you've given me your time

When you've given me that moment

When you've given me your kindness

When you've given me your support

When you've given me a lift

When you've given me your love.

Carol Kappes 2011

Loving You Is Wrong-

Because you are married
Because of the distance
Because of the age
Because of the lifestyle
Because of the differences
Because of the uncertainty
Because of the habits
Because of the difficulties
Because of the religion

But, I'll always love you!

Carol Kappes 2011

I'd Love To Snuggle With You. . .

In the car
   While we are driving to our latest vacation spot

In the theater
   While we are watching a romantic/adventure movie together

On the sofa
   As we communicate and talk about our day with each other

In the cave
   As we are walking through the mystery and stillness of the dark

In the stadium
   As we are watching our favorite sport and teams play

At the concert
   As it brings so much joy to hear music and to be here with you

In the camper
   As we make our evening meal together by moonlight and candle

At the amusement park
   As we take a ride on the roller coaster way up high

In the boat
   As we go for a cruise on the lake or the ocean

In the auditorium
   As we are watching the spectacular performance of the play

In the arena
   As we are watching the spectacular horse show

At the bus/train station
   As we make the journey back home from the trip

At the hospital/office
   When we are both looking and holding our newborn/adopted child

By the fireplace
   As we enjoy the warmth of the glowing fire log and embers

On the bench
   As we enjoy the view at the beach, park, meadow, or woodlands.

In the bed
   Underneath the blanket as we make passionate love to each other

Carol Kappes 2012
Inspired of affection
Dedicated to DAK

Love

A Love Bonded

There was an attraction
Between you and me
A bond that was meant to be.

Your cares and gentle touch
That I loved so much
Really meant the world to me.

It gave me the strength
That endured through time
Like a clock's enchanted chime.

Even 'til this day
Your love will always stay
Deep within my heart and mind.

Carol Kappes 1999
In Dedication to MP, MD
Published in 2000,"Season's of Life"
International Library of Poetry

Pleasure...

It's something we all seek-
It's the loving smile
It's the sparkling eye
It's the warm embrace
It's the intimate kiss
It's the sweet cuddle
It's the spoken words
It's the gentle touch
It's the foamy bath
It's the lighted candle
It's the bubbly champagne
It's the fancy dinner
It's the refreshing mint
It's the walk in the park
It's the hug in the moonlight
It's the cozy fireplace
It's the sensual glow
It's the romantic evening
It's the taste of lovemaking
It's something we all treasure-

Carol Kappes 2011
In Dedication to AC

Why Do You Play With My Heart?

You glanced and stole my heart,
Then your words just filled me-
I became overwhelmed by them.

Feelings of love were enhanced
At each moment of your touch
As your kindness overflowed.

I hear and see you in my mind
When I awake with each morn-
My heart aches for your love.

Tell me why you tug at my heart
I'm afraid to fall in love with you.
This could be just a lover's game.

It's filled with fun and excitement
That lasts for just a brief moment-
And happens once in a lifetime.

Carol Kappes 2011
Inspired of all suitors
In Dedication to VS

Your Love Ignites Me

Your thought has become...

A fire flame in my heart,
Glowing my mind,
Heating my feelings, and
Burning my soul!

I can't do without you because
You have total control of me...

I love you my love

"Secret Admirer" (written verse)
Carol Kappes (wrritten title)
In collaboration Aug, 2012
Carol's Corner

Roses Within

Roses of red grow in my heart
And they will never wither;

Cause they bloom every time...

I see your smile
Hear your voice or
Just think of you!

Carol Kappes (Written title)
An Admirer (Written verse)
In collaboration 2013
Inspired of dating/courting
Dedicated to BM

I Want Your Love

I want to get to;

Know you
Love you
Want you
Need you
Kiss you
Hold you
Feel you
Desire you
Excite you!

And never let you go.

Carol Kappes 2013
Inspired of Dating
Dedicated to C

On An Emotional Level . . .

I understand you a whole lot better
I learned how to enjoy and love you
I accepted your strength and weaknesses
I gained more knowledge about you
I felt your care, kindness, and laughter
I became connected with you
I admire you more and more each day
I know that you will always be near

Carol Kappes 2013
Dedicated to GF
Inspired of a deeper love
Within the relationship

Man's Desire Of Love

Is like a volcano-

It is rising, it is hot

Then it is...

Going to pulse
Going to move
Going to emerge
Going to flow
Going to heat
Going to erupt
Going to explode!

Carol Kappes 2013

Woman's Desire Of Love

Is like a tornado-

It is funnel-shaped, it is dense

Then it is...

Going to soften
Going to widen
Going to moisten
Going to increase
Going to pressure
Going to intensity
Going to ecstasy!

Carol Kappes 2013

Self

Thoughts

Where do they come from?
How does it make us feel?
Why do we have them?
When do they appear?
What distance are they?
How do we use them?

Some thoughts are blank
And some thoughts show pictures.
Some thoughts are good,
And some thoughts are bad.
Some thoughts stay with you,
And some thoughts are forgotten.

Your thoughts reflect you
And is determined by you:
"Who You Are"
"What You'll Be"
"Where You'll Go"
"What You'll Do"

Carol Kappes 2011
Inspired by a networking friend
Created in Macy's café
During my lunch

Serious

When you are a serious person
Some things get to your system.

You'd like things to be perfect
Even though it seems impossible.

You have to learn to adjust of
The circumstances that you face.

And the last month seemed difficult
So I'm giving myself a break.

Please hold firmly to your ideals
Until then, it's what you've become.

Carol Kappes 2012
Inspired of peoples' traits

Self-

Self-awareness
Self-business
Self-confidence
Self-determination
Self-esteem
Self-fulfillment
Self-gracious
Self-help
Self-image
Self-justice
Self-knowledge
Self-less
Self-made
Self-notion
Self-observant
Self-preservation
Self-query
Self-reliance
Self-sacrifice
Self -taught
Self-understanding
Self-vision
Self-will
Self-x chromosome
Self-yearn
Self-zeal

Carol Kappes 2013
Inspired of the ways you
Reach self-development
From the alphabet A-Z

R.E.

Recover
Relive
Relocate
Remake
Restart
Recapture
Rebuild
Reclaim
Refresh
Reborn
Regain
Restore
Reform
Reassess
Realign
Reinforce
Revitalize
Rebound
Rearrange
Reinvent
Recharge
Release
Restyle
Restructure
Redeem
Rethink
Redevelop
Relaunch
Refocus
Rejuvenate

Remind yourself to renew!

Carol Kappes 2013
Inspired of renewing oneself
After some loss/tragedy/divorce

What I Am. . .

Is because of what I listened to, learned and observed.

Is because of what I studied, read and watched.

Is because of what society/community had showed and demonstrated me.

Is because of what my choices, decisions and outcome had been.

Is because of what attitude, character and standards were important to me.

Is because of what certain people and pets brought into my life.

Carol Kappes 2013

A Messenger

Delivers the news

Has a voiced concern

Role of guidance

Relates information

Runs an errand

Bearer of delivery

Carol Kappes 2011

One Step Closer To God

Each year and you are
Closer to God and love

Carol Kappes (Written title)
Social Networker (Written verse)
In collaboration
Dedicated MG
Oct, 2013
Inspired of gaining an understanding
Into the spiritual world's existence

Discipline Creates:

Learning
Structure
Knowledge
Obedience
Organization
Routine
Function
Rules/Laws
Etiquette
Conduct
Manners
Ethics
Morals
Empathy
Character
Self-control
Choices
Willpower
Less stress
Compliant
Compromise
Agreement

Carol Kappes 2011
Inspired of better living

Life Is How You Make It

What are the ingredients? How do you begin to start? Where do we begin? What temperature does it require? How should we blend it together? Or is it stirred? Will it taste sweet or sour? What if it doesn't turn out? Then what do we do? Do we start over again?

How does it look? Is it baked yet or overly done? Touch the surface to see if it bounces back, or cooked just right. Does it seem tender or too dry? Shall we turn down the heat or turn up the heat? Which way should it go? I think it's just right. Let's take a look.

Does it look perfect for the palate? Is it pretty and delicious on the serving platter? Will the guests enjoy it? How can we tell? We can witness their conversation and pleasing gestures. We can ask them if they want more. Did they get plenty to eat? It looks like they are having a fun time.

Let's add the drinks. Are they too cold or just right? Does it have the bubbly sparkle in the glass? Is it colorful and quenches the thirst or is it bitter? Did we add the garnish or ice on top to make it pleasing and exciting? Was it served well?

How were the guests feeling? Did they have a good time, or were they a little shy? Did we take the time to introduce one another and make them feel welcome? If not, why not? The atmosphere had soft music playing, everyone liked the sound! It was pleasing and enchanting.

Did the guests leave with happy thoughts and well wishes? Did they enjoy your company? How does one know? You see the smiles and hear the goodbyes as they leave. They purposely came and said they had a great time. The imprint you left them is very lasting, so handle all your friends and guests with loving care and kindness!

Carol Kappes 2011

Take Out Of the World; What You Put Into It

You bring out a laugh...you feel good

You bring out a joy...you feel pleasure

You bring out a smile...you feel happy

You bring out a cry...you feel sad

You bring out a whine...you feel discontent

You bring out a talk...you feel connected

You bring out a sigh...you feel weary

You bring out a disgust...you feel terrible

You bring out a pain...you feel hurt

You bring out anger...you feel displeasure

You bring out anxiety...You feel nervous

Carol Kappes 2012

God's Love

My love of God
As you will see-
Comes only from within me.

It's in a place
Within my heart
Where it all began to start.

From the Holy Bible
When things were down;
I read without a frown.

It gave me peace
Understanding and love-
Words of wisdom from above.

Carol Kappes 2003

I Come To Realize:

That your life is planned out! I knew it since high school—I predicted something that would happen when I reached near a certain age and it did—In fact, I was so ill that my doctor couldn't sleep for his concern in me. (I had been in intensive care unit for a number of days with heart racing, collapsed lung) As I was healing, he asked, "What keeps me going?"

I told him thru prayers and faith. I was so sick, even watching TV was far from my mind—I only concentrated on getting better—

As I went thru the doorstep of my home, tears rushed down my face—knowing that I just about didn't have this chance. I realized I had more to do in life. (I had a home health care nurse take care of me for a week or two).

When I went to the surgeon's office for the health check, my doctor went straight to the waiting area to see my two children (unexpected). I knew then one reason why I had to live.

Ever since then, I view life at a different angle; for one reason it's because I'm still here and another reason is that I felt HIS presence and peace during my struggles in this life.

There are signs of his presence to this day; some are able to feel and see it and some cannot see. But HE does work in our lives; through our heart, mind, and soul if we only allow, notice or pay close attention to it—because He planned it out for us!

Carol Kappes 2011
(Inspired by 1998 Hospital
Intensive Care Unit –Major Surgery)
In Dedication to KS
And Many Who Believe in HIM

His Chosen People. . .

You're now one of 13 apostles
And none will question you.

"Social Networker" (Written verse)
Carol Kappes (Written title)
In collaboration
October, 2012

God

A Designed World

Some people tell me I live in a "dream" world
You know what? I tell them I live in a "God's" world

There is a difference

Would we have problems if we lived according to
His Plan?
If He came on Earth today
Would He ask, "What are we doing?"

His design was for us to obey, honor, and love Him
Is this too much to ask?

It's our thoughts, actions, and work that defines us
as humans

We were superior over the animals

If animals can obey man;
Why can't we obey God?

Carol Kappes 2012
(Religion variances of nations)
Written at library while on social media sites

Angels

They guide you
They protect you
They message you
They direct you
They tell you
They influence you
They lead you
They help you
They inform you
They love you

Carol Kappes 2011

Believe

If I told you that I live
With God's Holy Spirit

You wouldn't believe me.

If I told you that I live
Here on earth till death

You would believe me.

Many people seem to only
Believe in what they see;
Not in what they can't see!

So learn to trust in God as
He guides your direction.

Carol Kappes 2012
Inspired of Belief in God

Destiny

For you, Mom, with all my love—
May God's blessings come from above.

He grants you strength with each day
And guides your destiny in every way.

Looking back beyond all those years
There has been shed many tears.

But through it all, it made you strong
And God had been with you all along.

He's with you today, and always will be
Till his hands touch upon you for eternity!

Carol Kappes 1991
In Dedication to My Mother, RS
Entered Eternity in Sept, 2008

Divine Love-

Reaches out to you
Comforts you
Heals you
Consoles you
Helps you
Satisfies you
Blesses you
Guides you
Loves you
Protects you
Strengthens you
Lifts you
Nourishes you
Trusts you
Answers you
Encourages you
Cares for you
Touches you
Holds onto you
Motivates you
Inspires you
Hears you
Forgives you
Weeps with you
Watches over you

Carol Kappes 2011
Inspired of the "Greatest Love"
As in God's Love

Innocent Prayer

I'm asking in kindness
This innocent prayer,
To help me through
The days in my life.

A journey of hope
In this little prayer,
For the very best
That's offered to me.

A venture of love
In this sent prayer,
When special times
I will call unto you.

A guided direction
In this holy prayer,
To continue forever
In everything I do.

Carol Kappes 2012
Inspired by a friend
Thru networking
Dedicated to MI

Prayer: Brings You Close To God

To have a relationship with Him

To know and understand His will

To give Him thanks and praise

To worship and honor Him

To ask for assistance of Him

To ask for your forgiveness

To receive knowledge and wisdom

To hear His word more clearly

To live a more peaceful life

To prepare you for eternity

Carol Kappes 2011
(Variances in faith and religion by culture)

Reasons For a Prophet

To guide your path in righteousness

To help you reach eternity to heaven

To teach you all about God's will

To show your purpose of fulfillment

To live a meaningful and blessed life

To keep your insights on His glory

To feel a love that is everlasting

To have structure and course in life

To talk of wisdom and understanding

To teach knowledge and strength

To be aware of acts of sinfulness

To follow His guidance through life

To know His teachings and ways

Carol Kappes 2011
Inspired of faith
"From the Beginning of Time--
Past, Present and Future"

Prophetess

Your words are like the
The words of a prophet.

Telling parochial people
What truly matters on life.

Carol Kappes (Written Title)
Social Networker (Written Verse)
Dedicated to VG
In collaboration 2013

Our Life To Hold

There was one time in my life when I felt depressed.
I remember it was around junior high.

You know what I did? --------
I picked up the Bible. And read His Word.

It gave me hope-------
To want something and eventually it will be granted in time.

It gave me thankfulness--------
To learn to be grateful in life and don't take things for
granted.

It gave me strength-------
To know that in things we endure, we learn to pick ourselves
up and keep going.

It gave me wisdom-------
To know that knowledge is the beginning to understanding
your life.

It gave me love-------
To know the depth and meaning to the divine love that is
given to us.

It gave me faith-------
To believe and trust that all things are possible through Him.

It gave me life-------
To learn that the Spirit enhances our desire to be all that
we can be in life through knowing Him.

It gave me courage-------
To learn that when we go through difficulties in life; it
builds our character.

It gave me prayer-------
To take a moment each day and reflect upon; and give
thanks and praise to Him.

Carol Kappes 2011
Inspired of Despair and
Hopelessness in life

Soul

Stories told us we have one
Are we living up to it?
Do we strive for existence?

Are we having clear thoughts
Or is it somewhat stained?
Do we strive for success?

Are there any sacrifices
That we must offer up?
Do we strive for acceptance?

At the end of our earthly life
Were we prepared to die?
Do we strive to meet God?

Carol Kappes 2012
Inspired of death; end of life

Spiritual Love

It's unlike any other kind of love
Its hold is strong unto your heart
It's constantly flowing as a waterfall
It's smooth and sails so freely.

It's measured to the depths of grace
Its purity is like that of a diamond
It's received by those that are worthy
It's the signature of everlasting love.

Carol Kappes 2012
Dedicated to AM
Inspired by networking

This Light I See-

When I look at the unique candle flame
I seem to think of Christ's enduring light.

It is His light that shines to the world-
Darkness is an opposition to the light.

The world was made by God's design
And within the sun is a shining light.

Its purpose it to make people so aware that
Through their eyes; in hoping to see light-

The world would be the most prized possession,
When they view the beauty in spectrum light,

That they will forever treasure and behold the
Essence of the world; even in the moon's light.

Carol Kappes 2011
Inspired of creation,
Purpose and plan

Feel God's Love

God's love is like the

Ocean; vast and deep.

You can't ever see it,

But you can feel it.

Carol Kappes 2013
Inspired of the depth
Of God's love He gives.
Love is not seen, but felt.

The World Was Created By God

In the beginning; man had not been created
Then God had another plan:

God created man and woman to please Him;
Weakness brought separation of man from God.
Disobedience came into the world

In came the longing for God to have a son
Then God had another plan:

God brought forth His son named Jesus Christ;
Born into a stable for the salvation of souls.
Disbelief once again came into the world

In came the closeness for God to mankind
Then God had another plan:

God demonstrated that through His death;
We also are born in the likeness to Jesus Christ.
Descending within us His Holy Spirit

Carol Kappes 2013
Inspired of one true God
Who created the world

I Have Lived As Christ Seen. . .

I have been the woman who hemorrhaged
I have had children in my later years
I have known death of a 12 year old child
I have heard and understood my inner voice
I have had guardian angels watch over me
I have faced the devil in my life
I have observed we are all sinners
I have seen inheritance wasted
I have seen greed over priority
I have been through a betrayal
I have seen wickedness of men
I have understood the Lord's Prayer
I have acknowledged the Ten Commandments
I have seen the world in God's eyes
I have felt His eternal love
I have felt His unending peace
I have seen sorrow of women's tears
I have understood His will for me
I have had incisions and sutures in my body
I have endured and carried the crosses in my life
I have knowledge about my purpose and direction
I have accepted there is a God, Son, and Holy Spirit
I have viewed death as passing earth life to another

Carol Kappes 2012
Inspired of My Life;
Born into this world

Death; As An Arrow

Death, itself, is like an arrow. When the arrow
Leaves the bow from the archer's (God's)
Hands, it flees through quickly and is aimed
At one particular spot. The arrow strikes it
Down and it can no longer live. It becomes
Suddenly taken away and leaves a moment
Of bereavement and sadness to those around.

The embedded mark that is left of the arrow
Is often the memories and legacy that the
Person leaves behind. And how precious they
Seem to be!

Carol Kappes 1985
Inspired of death

Nation

Iraq

USA soldiers pulled out,
Take care of yourselves.

Find peace and comfort
After this long, enduring war.

Your road will begin for
Recovery to your nation.

Your people must be strong
And look forward to a future;

For progress, education and
Law-abiding citizens' welfare.

Carol Kappes 2011
Inspired by USA/IRAQ
War Ended after nine years

To Russia

Today I heard your people's cry,
Looking for justice to prevail.

Elections can turn out wrong,
When people are not righteous.

In many nations; people seek the truth
And the times without it, it will falter.

Corruption is like the wild weed,
It kills victory for a nation's need.

Carol Kappes 2012
Inspired by actual events

For Iran

Like in a divorce, the many
Hurts can be swept away.
What was in the past,
Is no longer in the present.

Like a woman on her own,
She carries stamina each day.
What was in the mind,
Is no longer in her heart.

Like a burden that it was
The load seems lighter today.
What was in the past,
Is no longer in the present.

Carol Kappes Sept, 2013
Inspired of the telephone conversation of
USA Pres. Obama and Iran Pres. Rouhani
(The needs of today; is different from the past.)

Syria

Syria in a long, enduring conflict;
This does not make any sense.
How can a "leader" be so cruel
And watch thousands killed to death?

You have no shame or guilt? Or is
This the way you view human life?
Put yourself in harm's way and
Get the "feel" of torment and evil.

Put an end to this atrocity now-
Shelter the rest from this storm.
Work compassion into your soul
So that others can live in dignity.

Carol Kappes 2013
Inspired of Syria civil war

Egypt Uprising

Freedom
Liberty, rights
Exclaiming, rejoicing, smiling
Proud people making choices
Freedom

Carol Kappes 2011
Inspired by actual events in nations

People Have Fled Syria

I know how you feel-

You feared for your own lives
You face suffering and pain
You are abandoned and scared
You are hungry, thirsty and cold
You are discouraged and sad
You feel neglected and unloved
You are desperate and cry
You are worried and helpless
You are sick and weakened

God didn't want this; the
Fault of people did this.

Carol Kappes 2013
Inspired of the people who had
To flee due to human error.

India

It's still a foreign land to me
That I, eventually, want to see.

I have made lots of friends today;
And there's so much I'd like to say.

They've asked me about my future;
If a trip to India was planned for sure.

It's something I'd really love to do-
I thought about it many times, too.

Over half the world away, they've shown
Me their culture; which became known.

A friendship that became so true;
It's been a pleasure to meet you.

As I have to finally say "Goodbye"
Back in the states, I'll again say "Hi."

Carol Kappes 2011
Inspired by LinkedIn networking friends
First Connection of foreign nation from India
And to all foreign countries around the World.

Entering a Foreign Nation, You Notice-

The accent/language of the people during the flight
The physique of the people in the country
The food and beverages that they eat and drink
The portion sizes of the meals and drinks
The cars/bus of transportation and license plate
The models and which side is the steering wheel
The direction of the way they travel
The difference to the streets and markings
The buildings and the scenery of trees; land
The underground trains and then walk to area
The way the transportation is designed in city
The way the behavior or attitude is of the people
The way of power outlets and toilets are designed
The way of the currency and the metric system used
The landmarks and sites of history for tourists
The clothing and hairstyles that people have
The food, products and design of the marketplace

(And this list goes on and on....)

Carol Kappes 2011
Inspired from visit to foreign land
On First International Flight

Holiday

Valentine's Greeting

Thoughts of love and happy smiles
From all of us across the miles.

We may be far apart in distance
But our hearts, in an instant-

Flutter you a Valentine's Day greeting
Of memories that are worth keeping!

With love,

Carol Kappes 1987

It's Our First Christmas Together

Just you and me
    Exchanging our gifts with happiness
        The love that came to be.

We're touched with pride
    As we travel throughout our life
        Walking side by side.

The magical scene
    Of that very first Christmas
        Reflects in you and me.

A brand new start
    With every passing day
        Begins inside our heart.

Carol Kappes 1986

My Christmas Card to You-2011

Wishing all of my friends
From around the globe
A glorious Christmas season!

Love is sent thru this card
To every corner of the world.
You mean so much to me.

Thanks so much for your love;
And I have loved you too.
We had a wonderful year-

I wish that Christ's peace
Will touch your lives forever
As HE had did for me.

Stay safe, happy, and healthy
This holiday season and more;
The world is perfect with love!

Happy holidays!
Yours truly,

Carol Kappes
Carol's Corner
State of Minnesota,
United States of America

Christmas so Bright (2012)

Christmas decorations all so bright
In the glistening snow of white
On this wintery cold night

It is an awesome, beautiful sight
When you see the blinking light
On this wintery cold night

Families gathered around so tight
For the meal to soon take plight
On this wintery cold night

Thoughts went to the Savior's might
The reason for peace and not to fight
On this wintery cold night

Carol Kappes 2012
Carol's Corner
State of Minnesota
United States of America

Greetings to all of you this Christmas and
Wishing you all happiness, joy, peace and love!

Does the Sun Set In the West and Rise In the East?

Jesus Christ is the Light of the World,
And He was born in the Eastern World;
A Savior to all of mankind. God had
Chosen this certain place; in the East.

We were to follow this certain star into
The evening sky; because the sun reads
Only time, not the land location. The star
Had shown brightness that evening night.

Jesus brings us PEACE in the darkest days
And nights. A comfort within our souls; we
Are in the likeness of Him. And His teachings
Live on throughout the West and the East.

Remember that the light of the sun rises in the
Eastern horizon, reaches high above at noon;
And by evening it sets in the Western horizon.
We all must share in the Light of Jesus Christ.

Carol Kappes 2013 (Written verse)
Social networker (Written title)
Dedicated to PTL
Inspired that the Son of God came to
All people in all nations of the world
As the Savior (Salvation) to mankind

Thanksgiving Vacation

I want to thank my many connections,
Readers, friends, family, and loved
Ones for your continued, loving support.

I am taking holiday vacation to reflect
Thanks and praise to our God for the
Many blessings upon each of us and
Also for our future generations to come.

We see the magnificent beauty in the
World. Man must continue to keep it that
Way, our responsibility to behold.

Carol Kappes 2013
Inspired of Thanksgiving
To give thanks to others

A New Year, 2012

Off to begin another new year
We will be happy, my dear!
Going full speed, without fear
To witness history soon near.

Chances are we'll have to hear
Or see some news that brings a tear.
But courage and strength will sear
Any difficulty that happens to appear.

What is really important to our ear
If we had heard it from our peer-
Is that no matter what is in the gear,
We made it the best of any one year!

Carol Kappes 2011

A New Year, 2014

Bring out the best in YOU
And pass it on to others!

A champagne toast will be
A great way to start.

Carol Kappes 2013

Interview

War and Its Emotional Effects

"these days my brother was mortally wounded in 1992..."

Can you briefly tell me what he said in the letter that is vital for us to know? What do you remember as IMPORTANT in the words that he left for you?

"in wounds on the battlefield lying wounded..."

You sound very hurt from this terrible war? It must have been so bad

"worse than you think..."
"what about the novel that I possess"

Tell me of your novel?

"this is unpublished novel about the war in bosnia"
"i want to publish in USA, need a publisher"

Are you writing this?

"it is written in the war in war conditions"

Your brother left this behind you told me earlier, now I remember Bosnia sounds like a great name for your country!

"bosnia sounds like carol"
"history says that bosnia was three"

Has it been published in your country? To tell of the pain?

"no"
"THE RISKS TO FAMILIES. My opinion"

Carol Kappes 2012 (My VOICE unquotes)
Social networker (His VOICE in quotes)
In collaboration; inspired by chat dialogue
He is from Bosnia and Herzegovina area

I Do Care; For Your Happiness

"I love the time spent with you on internet,
As you have been a source of care and
Happiness to me in my tough days,
I hope we will keep this relationship forever.

God bless you, take care of yourself and
Your family,
Regards,"

Believe me; I do not forget anyone of you with
Whom I have spoken. You will be with me
Always in your heart; and don't take this away.
It has to do with the Spirit; and I feel that in you.

Love,

Carol Kappes April, 2013
In collaboration
E-mail conversation with
Linkedin networker in quotes
Dedicated to IA
Inspired of caring for others

Receiving the Holy Spirit

"You are one of the few persons who brought a great positivity in my life, due to your presense, I have reasons to believe that much can be done with the pure will and the pure heart! I will always need your support!"

You know what that is? It is the Holy Spirit within you. It is God, Son and Holy Spirit. I believe in this and I know it also. Yes, I plan to be there all my life with you...I already have you in my heart as well.

"Thank you so much for being with me, do you have any plan to be here?"

At the moment I have hospital bills to keep up with...I know...if only

"Not a problem, let's hope for it in the future."

Carol Kappes 2013
In collaboration
Dedicated to STHB
E-mail conversation with
Networker in quotes from
LinkedIn & Google plus
Social networking sites
March, 2013

Focus

"A guy wants to feel like you are focusing
On HIM, not some other man."

Oh, he surely will get FOCUSED on the
More he treats her RIGHT!

Carol Kappes 2013
A connection (Written in Quotes)
In Collaboration
Inspired of men/women divorced and
What they seek in the next relationship

When Others Can Describe
Your Personality

(Networker voice in quotes, Carol voice in non-quotes, edited)

"Dear Carol

Thank you for inviting me to your blog. I found it really interesting, instructive and tells a lot about your personality and how you perceive life and those around you. I am really proud of you and so blessed to know someone like you, knowledgeable and well versed in seminal subjects.

I am so interested in your blog and will always follow what you kindly post."

And I was a simple girl! Thank you so much! Yes, others are able to see my personality.

"You know dear Carol Ralph Waldo Emerson said that: *"Nothing is more simple than greatness; indeed, to be simple is to be great."* Moreover, *simplicity makes beauty. It is because you are a humble person with great potentials that you are talking about simplicity .On general terms, sophisticated people who have a wide range of knowledge tend to be the most modest of all, while empty barrels, or those with a little knowledge, make the most noise.*

 I, therefore, strongly encourage you in your path and wish you all the best of luck. I am indeed very proud of you and highly praise your human values and principles."

Thank you for those thoughts. (I asked him what faith he was; for my understanding) Then I talked a little on my divorce.

"I am so sorry to hear that you have been through those hard times and ordeals. We all experience hard times in our life but we need to be strong enough to come out victorious and with the least wounds possible, so that we can keep up and continue our path in life.

Having said that, I can sense a lot determination and strength in your message that's why I am proud of you again because of your strong personality and your clinging to life no matter what happens. After all, life must go on regardless. I do really love your personality that can be a source of inspiration and hope."

Thanks…yes…feedback helps me get better at what I do for sure. I am an emotional/expressive writer that wants to get to the heart n soul of people. And that is also how I chat/interview with others. Many times I get more ideas from doing that.

"It is so true when you said that feedback from people helps you get better and at the same time feedback gives you some insightful ideas that reshape your thinking and enable you to share with your readers your diverse experiences and stories in life and about life."

Yes…likewise I see all these diverse cultures in my dental office…so I see people of all colors the same. They have all the basic needs to live. To keep healthy n live.

"Yes, so true!!! No matter what our skin color, our background or religion are, we are all human beings, belonging to the same race, with one God, the Creator and Almighty above everyone, anything and everything on earth.

You are lucky enough to meet people from different cultures and backgrounds, who all have the same hopes, same objectives, same likings, and most importantly, they do share the same human universal values.

I wish you the best of luck in your brilliant and inspiring career."

I'll have to use your last sentence here when I market my goal of a book when I get that finalized!

"I will be the first one to have the honor and privilege of buying your book. When is it gonna come out??"

Working on manuscript thus now…then look for a publisher.

And how old are you? I am around (5 yr range) yrs old. But I look 10 yrs younger then my actual age. (I ask their age so I am informed of the generation they are in)

"Indeed, you look much younger than that range of age dear Carol. The most important thing is that I see in your pictures, a very young lady, full of spring, full of energy, full of dynamism and most importantly, full of hope, optimism and much much more joy and happiness.

A young and talented lady (indeed so gifted), with a very young spirit and a lovely and a lively mode of living, that can be so inspiring to those who are young in age, but old in spirit…those who have lost hope in life…those who have been repressed and frustrated in life, because of so many ordeals and bad luck.

I can see in you a young woman who is proud of herself, who has a high self esteem and self confidence and a woman who is smart enough to be a role model for others. In short, you are a young spirited woman, so Kind-hearted and with high potentials and a wide range of knowledge in life."

First of all I want to tell you that you described me well…and known me in one day…wow.

"I am so delighted that I was successful in describing to some extent your true being, personality and your physical appearance."

Carol Kappes 2014
(Interview)
Dedicated to KG
Inspired how others perceive you.
Make the best of YOU.

Interview Of Islam
and Christian Faith

(Social Networker voice in quotes; Carol Kappes voice in non-quotes)

POST INTERVIEW

Well, I did sleep; but got up way too late than I wanted to. Wed is my day off. You definitely will go down in history of 5 hours of "interview" time that I ever had. This gave me a glimpse also of how you think of Jesus; which I believe may be the factor of "problems" in this world that people do not believe in Him; but I am not a scholar and no one ever was able to come to the conclusion why people "act out" in this part of the world.

This is what I am trying to figure out in a sort of way; I would love for it to end in some treaty so people's lives are not in CHAOS. The world was never made for that.

But we all know life is unjust and always was…

"I just want you to check where the truth doesn't mater is how many years you Learn it or you practice all of us we just looking for truth.
People before Jesus when Jesus came to them and he ask then to follow his way and he tell them this the troth from Gad

What they answer to him? They said to him we have so many years learn & follow & practice our own way and our father and grandfather way and you want us to change it and follow you??!!

I mean here that's if you was learn and follow and practice something this doesn't mean is it the truth."

I have learned, followed and practice in what I know the possible way; and it is to understand the truth. I do believe that I have a great understanding; but I will never know the reality of it all. How could I? You are right, it may be impossible for anyone to exactly know all circumstances to the Word of God. Even his own apostles sometimes questioned and wondered.

One of them betrayed Jesus and Jesus also knew ahead of time which one that was going to be. Jesus was a visionary or he heard from God his Father? Sometimes you have to believe, even though you can't see him.

THE INTERVIEW

Man has destroyed humans by killings, abortions, etc than God does by natural disasters.

"What about the people befor Jesus came?"

The people before Jesus were just the same probably; some believe and others didn't
All of man would have changed the religions from the very first religion
And I don't know what that first religion really is

I think humans destroy more people than disasters do
Do I make sense to you?

"ok, if God have son and he send his son to do goal in earth with the people the Q is why a God powerful why not save his son?"

God and Jesus could have saved himself, but, the reason that He didn't was that he had to fulfill the scriptures from the old testament. I guess in the old testament it was forthcoming. But which ones I would not know.

"And save his goal if not retch this goal, why god send him as son?"

??Not sure what you are asking here? It was the people that were unbelievers to Jesus. Remember the Ceasar crowd and some did not want Jesus hung on the cross? About half of the people or more believed he was the King of the Jews. After he died, more thought he really was and Jesus death on the cross represent our crosses to bare. We don't have life easy, I feel my life was a lot like Jesus, really I do.

"The reson to have a son what? To save pepole from sins right? Did Jesus do it did he continued so the people kill him and his father watch that when he powerfull and the aim will not be done so what the resone to send son for something not done? The people are controlling God and son of god."

That was an interesting statement you wrote. But I come up with the fact that people remained disobedient, disbelief; just as when the world was made.

"the God is one and Jesus is normal prophet with mircal and god is powerful he do whatever he want and we all believing thats."

Wow

"in Islam when the people going to kill him God pull him in the sky"

Kill who in Islam? Oh Jesus?
"Yes"

Interesting. I know many people do not live in faith. Why did you want to know my thinking on this? It was scholarly work on my part.

"What the logic here why God not save his son in Islam God save Jesus and take him to sky?"

I think one reason is that Jesus might have had to go to hell. In which he did descent then He went up to heaven

"You know the person was killed in the crose?"

There were 3 that day, 2 prisoners with Jesus. And Jesus told the prisoner, you will be with me in paradise. So we will see and hear the judgement. Anyway, this is a lot of thinking on my part. You really had everything checked out with me. Very interesting. Did I make this sensible to you? This is all my belief. We touched on many subjects in one short day?

"Yes, but just last the person who was killed in crose is the one who bring food to Jesus he informed the people which they need about his place so God take Jesus make the face."

Wow

"Make the face of the man same face of Jesus so the people take this man as Jesus and kill him."

I don't think that would have been done

"why God can't do thats?"

Because of God's apostles, another reason he needed witnesses. Did they prepare his body for burial? And then rolled the stone and they kept an eye on his grave

"Yes"

Till they seen that he rise as he told his apostles he would and they did see him when he descended from hell to go to heaven

"Jesus never go to hell."

He had to. I think he did because we are born of his likeness.

"What he done wrong to be in hell?"

He is like us. He had to experience it. Maybe to tell us there is a heaven and hell.

"How his son of God and how he will be in hell?"

I'm not sure that part in Bible or if that is from the catholic teachings. I would have to look this up. It could be catholic.

"See, Jesus in Islam is a Holy and Mary she is a Holy and God make a miracal to us to see us do we believe him or not."

I believe what all I told you and it comes from my knowledge. But I had read the new testament in high school age. And went to church when I grew up.

"Can I see you now?" (use of webcam)

"I can see you are Religion women"

Well I would describe myself as spiritual

"The knowledge you have."

I am not holy but I do believe that Jesus planned and is running my life. He gives me these thoughts ahead, I am visionary. I make choices from those thoughts. I write from my mind, the earthly experience and the spiritual world. I can no longer develop myself; I am now developing others

"Yes, all what you said now is right. But all that's for the God not son"

Have you heard of Maslow's theory? I have accomplished what
I needed in myself but I am transcending to help Gen X and Y
through social networking and the internet. God as his son is in
heaven and left his spirit to me.

"Can I see you please" (use of webcam)

But I seem to think of Jesus more in my life due to the fact he was
human like I am. I live for God; I see the world in God's eyes. I see
how he created it and how he wanted it to be.

(Then on came the webcam)

Carol Kappes 2013 (Written in non-quotes)
A social networker (Interviewed; Written in quotes)
In collaboration
Dedicated to SE
Inspired of Various Religion and Beliefs about Jesus Christ
(I had spoken to at least three Muslim men about their faith.
They were very similar to this conversation)

Photo by Heikkila Studios, Farmington, MN

About the Author

Carol Kappes, an emotional/expressive writer, is currently an "Author of Verse" on Carol's Corner at Carolkappes.blogspot.com. She has written posts on various aspects to life and has acquired a world-wide audience; within her third year. The concept to the writing pieces came about from social networking at LinkedIn and Google plus. In her freelance writing, Carol has the ability to plan and envision that her writing can bring purpose and meaning to people's lives.

Carol is a resourceful, accomplished and dedicated licensed dental assistant professional with over 30 years of four-handed and expanded functions dentistry. Carol is described as a team member, who sets high standards, and is committed to excellence. She currently holds the position working for pediatric and general dentists.

Carol was born in Iowa, the daughter of a farmer and lived on the family farm. She attended public schools and graduated from New Hampton High School, IA. Upon graduation, her interest had taken her to Rochester, MN where she graduated from Rochester Community and Technical College with diploma in Dental Assisting and acquired the MN Registered Dental Assistant license.

Carol continued with her career at dental offices in Iowa, California (1984-1992) and Minnesota (2002-Present). On-going continuing education, training, and seminars have been a part of her career. MN Board of Dentistry has recognized the career advancement and now changed this degree to Licensed Dental Assistant.

Carol currently resides in Apple Valley, MN. She has been married, divorced, and raised two children whom are now young adults.

www.ingramcontent.com/pod-product-compliance
Lightning Source LLC
Chambersburg PA
CBHW020435130626
46549CB00001B/152